Number Four: The Centennial Series of the
Association of Former Students
Texas A&M University

SECOND FATHERLAND

The Life and Fortunes of a German Immigrant

Max A. P. Krueger at age seventy-three.

SECOND FATHERLAND

The Life and Fortunes of a German Immigrant

By

MAX AMADEUS PAULUS KRUEGER

Edited with an introduction by

MARILYN MCADAMS SIBLEY

Texas A&M University Press

COLLEGE STATION AND LONDON

Library of Congress Cataloging in Publication Data

Krueger, Max, 1851–1927.
    Second Fatherland.

    (The Centennial series of the Association of
Former Students, Texas A & M University; no. 4)
    Published in 1930 under title: Pioneer life in
    Texas.
    Includes index.
    1. Frontier and pioneer life—Texas. 2. Ranch life
—Texas. 3. German Americans—Texas. 4. Texas—
Biography. 5. Krueger, Max, 1851–1927. I. Title. II.
Series: Texas. A & M University, College Station.
Association of Former Students. The Centennial
series of the Association of Former Students, Texas
A & M University; no. 4.
F391.K94 1976   976.4'004'31[B]   76-17539
ISBN 0-89096-017-8 (cloth) / ISBN 1-58544-061-2 (pbk.) /

Manufactured in the United States of America
First Paperback Edition

To the memory of
Carl C. "Polly" Krueger

Contents

Illustrations

All photographs courtesy of Carl C. Krueger, Jr.

Introduction

WHEN Max Amadeus Paulus Krueger wrote his memoirs at age seventy-four, he represented both an era and a dream. As a sixteen-year-old boy in delicate health, he had worked his way from Germany to Texas, arriving in 1868 when the state was in the throes of Reconstruction. In the decades that followed, he saw the state transformed from a frontier to an industrial society. Land where he had hunted mustangs became cottonfields; wild cattle he had gathered for the long drive gave way to blooded stock; Indian tribes who had terrorized his home dwindled to pathetic remnants on distant reservations. Barbed wire, railroads, oil gushers, and increased population changed the face of the land so that when he looked back from the perspective of half a century he realized that he lived in a different world.

Krueger not only saw the transformation but participated in it. As an almost penniless immigrant, he yearned to be a rancher. He worked as stevedore, well-digger, factory hand, miller, cowboy, photographer, merchant, or whatever other occupation presented itself until he achieved his goal. By the time he reached middle age, he owned ten thousand acres of land watered by the Guadalupe and Blanco rivers. He leased an additional five thousand acres and numbered his cattle and sheep in the thousands.

But the land that had given him his heart's desire also took it away. In the mid-1890's a drought gripped Texas. The Guadalupe River dried to a string of puddles and then to a barren waste. Over one-half of his cattle died, and prices dropped so low that livestock he sent to market scarcely paid the transportation. In the early stages of the drought, Krueger borrowed money on his land to feed his cattle, so when the rains still failed, he lost his ranch along with his herds. He found himself again in roughly the same straits as when he first landed in Texas, but with one difference: he was forty-eight years old with a large family to support.

Again he accepted whatever employment was available, working briefly as insurance agent and realtor. Then his luck returned. Becoming representative for a machine company that specialized in cotton gin machinery, he learned the business and in short order formed his own company. About the same time, the Spindletop gusher brought a new economic era to Texas. Krueger added oil well machinery to his production list and within a few years amassed a fortune far larger than the one he had lost. Thus he twice realized the American Dream. The experience left him with a love for his adopted land and faith in hard work that became running themes in his memoirs. His "Salutation," drawn from later portions of the book, isolates these themes. "No obstacle is too great but that it can be overcome by courage, perseverance, and the use of those gifts which the Creator has implanted within us," he wrote. "No man need despair in this blessed country of ours, even in the depths of poverty."

Although Krueger was too successful to be typical, he represented the immigrant of his era in many respects. Born at Griefswald in the German state of Mecklenburg on December 27, 1851, he was the youngest child of Dorathea Bremer and Carl Erdman Krueger. His father, an architect, died when Max was nine months old, leaving the family in straitened circumstances. His mother worked as seamstress and milliner to support her children—Matilda, Carl, and Max—but the two boys were thrust upon their own resources at tender ages. Carl, nine years Max's senior, went to sea at age fourteen, migrated to Texas, enlisted in the Confederate Army, and temporarily lost touch with the family. Max, after showing himself a precocious student at Kaiser Wilhelm Gymnasium in Berlin, served a year in the Prussian army, and was apprenticed at age fourteen to a silk merchant. Two years later, suffering from consumption and warned by his doctor to seek a warmer climate, he followed his brother to Texas, going by way of France, Spain, Cuba, and New Orleans.[1]

By the time Krueger arrived, Texas already had a significant German population.[2] In the early 1840's a group of German noble-

---

[1] Biographical information about Krueger has been derived from Carl C. Krueger, comp., *The Family of Max A. and Emilie Buergener Krueger* (San Antonio, Texas, 1965); M. Krueger, "Some Notes for My Children," unpublished manuscript in Carl C. Krueger, Jr., Collection, Rockport, Texas; and family letters, also in the Krueger Collection.

[2] Terry Jordan, *German Seed in Texas Soil* (Austin: University of Texas Press, 1967), p. 57, estimates that 41,000 inhabitants, or 7.3 percent of the total white population of Texas, was of German stock in 1870. See also Gilbert

men organized the Adelsverein to promote colonization there. Economic distress in that period prompted thousands of farmers to emigrate, and the abortive revolutions of 1848 sent a sprinkling of liberal intellectuals to join them. These attracted other German immigrants throughout the 1850's and still others after the interruption of the Civil War. By Krueger's time, San Antonio had so large a German population that the street signs were written in German as well as in Spanish and English, and towns such as Fredericksburg and New Braunfels were almost entirely German. Usually the Germans retained their language and culture and formed self-contained enclaves in the predominantly Anglo-American state. Usually, too, they were highly praised by out-of-state visitors. Frederick Law Olmsted waxed enthusiastic about their thrift, industry, and farming methods when he visited in 1857, and Edward King echoed the praises when he visited in 1874.[3]

Despite the sobering influence of Krueger's fellow countrymen, the land to which he came was conditioned to violence. The state had never been tamed except on the edges, and in 1868 the disorders of Reconstruction overlay those of the frontier. Krueger saw the violence firsthand. At the riproaring town of Helena, he saw men who never parted with their six-shooters and Bowie knives even when dancing and who settled their differences by the Helena duel—that is, the combatants' left hands were tied together and each man was given a stubby knife for the right; then they fought until one bled to death. At San Saba, where he made his first home, he saw the victims of an Indian massacre and helped make coffins to bury them. At Fredericksburg, where he moved when San Saba became too uncivilized, he was caught in a cattlemen's war and barely escaped when a companion was murdered.

The Texas Krueger first knew was also in the heyday of the open-range cattle industry, and that too he experienced firsthand. His imagination, like that of countless boys of his generation and later, was fired by the life of the cowboy. He saved his money until

G. Benjamin, *The Germans in Texas: A Study in Immigration* (Austin: Jenkins Publishing Co., 1974), pp. 55–65.

[3] See Frederick Law Olmsted, *A Journey Through Texas* (New York: Mason Brothers, 1859), pp. 169–214; and Edward King and J. Wells Champney, *Texas: 1874* (Houston: Cordovan Press, 1974), pp. 81–84.

he could buy the appropriate equipment and then headed for the cattle camps. When he looked back over his life, he recalled his interlude as a cowboy more vividly than any other—the dangers of racing through a stormy night after a stampeding herd, the weariness of the drive when dust from countless hooves parched the mouth and nose, the magic of nights around the campfire when a Negro cook played the guitar while Mexican herdsmen danced the fandango.

Krueger's zest for life eased his way in the new country, enabling him to savour to the fullest every experience, good or bad. He hunted buffalo along the Concho River and gathered freshwater pearls from the San Saba. He learned how to tell time by moonlight, how to jerk beef, and how to track game in the wilderness, and he became acquainted with the rattlesnake, tick, boll weevil, and javelina.

His health returned, and before his nineteenth birthday he acquired a wife—sixteen-year-old Emily Buergener, daughter of Karoline Gerlach and Friedrich Buergener. His in-laws, thrifty farmers who had emigrated from Waldeck in 1861, bitterly opposed the match, and as matters developed, his family also opposed it. The youthful marriage was beset by other hardships. Max and Emily suffered extreme poverty during their early years together, and two babies died at birth during the first two years. But despite the difficulties, the marriage endured. They became the parents of sixteen children, twelve of whom—seven boys and five girls—lived to maturity. After his ultimate success, Max built Emily a handsome house in San Antonio. There they celebrated their fifty-sixth wedding anniversary, and there she died in 1949, aged ninety-five, having survived him by twenty-two years.[4]

Krueger's involvement with the land—its beauty and brutality—pervades his book, and some of the changes he saw left him angry. An early conservationist, he recalled with dismay the deliberate burning of great cedar forests, the disappearance of the wild turkey, and the transformation of the San Saba River from a clear, crystal stream to a shallow one heavy with top soil. Ironically, his own career embodies the greatest threat to the environment—the coming of industrialization. As a new arrival he helped build the

[4] C. C. Krueger, comp., *Family of Max . . . Krueger*, n. p.

first meatpacking plant at Indianola; later, wherever he went, he built sawmills, flour mills, and cotton gins; and he found his eventual success in the manufacture of oil well equipment.

Krueger met a kindred spirit when Theodore Roosevelt visited San Antonio to recruit the Rough Riders for the Spanish American War. Not only were both men ahead of their time in regard to conservation, but both also had been sickly boys who went west in search of health and both treasured their adventures as cowboys. Roosevelt was amazed to learn that Krueger had eleven children and jokingly asked for a picture of the family when the number reached an even dozen. After Roosevelt became president and after the birth of baby Marguerite, Krueger complied with the request. Roosevelt acknowledged the picture with a letter on White House stationery that became one of the family's keepsakes, and for a time the picture hung in the White House.

Krueger, again like Roosevelt, was a chauvinistic American; unlike the Rough Rider, however, he had another country with claim to his loyalty. Krueger never wavered in his devotion to his adopted land, but he remained forever German. "The yearning for the Fatherland never dies out in the heart of the German immigrant," he wrote. He took a German-born wife; the German language was spoken in his home; and he returned time and again to his native land. But Krueger's Germany was far different from the one created by Otto von Bismarck. Indeed, Krueger emigrated two years before Bismarck united Germany with blood and iron under the auspices of Prussia. Rather than a goose-stepping, militaristic nation, Krueger remembered a land where children believed in fairies and adults did not altogether disbelieve.

Krueger alludes only briefly to World War I in his reminiscences. Once he comments almost wistfully that if the German vote in the United States were as united as the Irish, the nation would never have entered the war. And again, he speaks with pride of his son Carl Clifton, who graduated from Texas A & M University, entered the United States Army, and rose to the rank of major. Undoubtedly, the war brought heartache to Krueger, for his sister had married an official in the Kaiser's government and a young kinsman had died for the Kaiser in an early battle.[5] But there was no

[5] M. Krueger, "Some Notes," p. 1.

division in his loyalties. His youngest daughter recalls his staunchly pro-American stand. "This is my country and it has been good to me," he announced when the United States entered World War I, and, when a fellow immigrant voiced sympathies for Germany, he promptly squelched her, suggesting that she should return there if those were her sentiments.[6] After the war ended, however, he renewed his ties—both business and personal—with Germany, visiting there almost every year.

Krueger devoted the first two decades of the twentieth century to building his company, the San Antonio Machine & Supply Company. By 1920 he could boast of a company with $1 million in capital, $645,000 in surplus, and plants in Corpus Christi, Waco, and San Antonio. But once having achieved success, he began planning for the transfer of responsibility to his sons. He initially groomed Paul, his third son, to head the company, but Paul died of influenza during the 1918 epidemic. Krueger then chose Carl, his sixth son, for the task. Handing the reins of the business to Carl in 1920, Krueger traveled extensively, spent long vacations in Germany, and indulged in a passion for collecting paintings.[7]

While visiting in Germany in the summer of 1927, he slipped in a bathtub and suffered a concussion from which he died on September 28. In view of the narrow escapes of his early life, the manner of his death was ironic, but that he died in his native land was appropriate. Just as appropriately, his ashes were returned to Texas.[8]

Krueger wrote his memoirs during a vacation in Germany in 1924. "I so far have arranged to have my book—240 pages—printed in German in Frankfort," he wrote Carl. "It's taken me 30 days to write it. . . . I need about a dozen photos for illustrations which I shall have to take in Texas. This will delay the printing until February."[9]

But the printing was delayed longer than he expected. At the time of his death, the book was still unpublished. Krueger had written in the German language and for a German audience, but after

6 Interview with Mrs. Marguerite Krueger Parks, San Antonio, Texas, August 25, 1975.
    7 See *The Krueger Collection in the University Library* (College Station, Texas: Texas A&M University, n.d.).
    8 Parks interview, August 25, 1975.
    9 M. Krueger to C. C. Krueger, July 30, 1924, Krueger Collection.

his death, his son Carl recognized the value of the book to American audiences. He had the memoirs translated into English and published a limited edition of five hundred copies under the title *Pioneer Life in Texas* (San Antonio, 1930). These copies he gave to friends and business associates, and, as the decades passed, the book became a collectors' item that was seldom offered even by rare book dealers. In order to make the memoirs more generally available, Carl C. Krueger gladly agreed to the publication of this new edition by the newly established press of his alma mater. The book was in progress when he himself died in the summer of 1975.

In addition to the published memoirs, Max A. P. Krueger left some manuscript notes for his children which give details, primarily about the family, that were omitted from the published version. These notes, as well as family pictures, were made available by Carl C. Krueger, Jr., who took up where his father left off in the preparation of the book. In the present edition, details from the manuscript notes have been added to the text at the most appropriate point and are indicated by italics. Some slight rearrangement has been made of material that was obviously out of context, and some chapters have been retitled or redrawn to indicate the subject more correctly and give better balance.

Krueger is sometimes hazy about dates, understandably so, as he wrote years after the event, and on some minor points his manuscript notes differ from the published memoirs. Even so, his account describes, as he intended, the life, fortunes, and contributions of a German immigrant of the late nineteenth century.

Marilyn McAdams Sibley

SECOND FATHERLAND

The Life and Fortunes of a German Immigrant

NOTE

Details from Krueger's additional manuscript notes, described by the editor in the introduction, have been added in italics to the original text at appropriate points.

Salutation

I have tried to describe faithfully in these chapters the life and fortunes of a German immigrant. All I have wished to prove was the simple truth that no obstacle is too great but that it can be overcome by courage, perseverance, and the use of those gifts which the creator has implanted within us. No man need, therefore, despair in this blessed country of ours, even in the depths of poverty.

Everything in this world is subject to change. At the age of forty-eight I had to begin working anew for strangers. After I had given up my properties, I rode to the summit of the beautiful Twin Sisters Ranch to take a last farewell of the wide expanse of land that I had called my own for twenty-five years and where I had spent my best energies and the happiest days of my life. Torturing doubts as to whether I still had the courage and energy to endure this kind of life beset my soul. I went back in memory to the time I entered this country and reviewed my life in a series of mental pictures, showing all the advantages gained, all the losses sustained during this long interval, and proved that my life's work had not benefited myself alone, but also the land of my choice. My courage rose with the rising sun, and I resolved to begin the struggle for a life worth living with renewed courage and energy. Animated by this thought, I put spurs to my horse and, singing with a glad voice the following passage from "The Beggar Student,"

Fate, your worst now do.

I shall die or conquer you!

I descended the mountains and began a new life.

If I have been able to inspire some of the younger generation with that indomitable courage that is indispensable for a successful struggle against the adversities of life; if I have induced some of the aged to remain in the land of their fathers and be content with existing conditions; and, finally, if I have succeeded in painting a truthful and accurate picture of the good old days that are no more; then I can lay down my pen and say goodbye with the satisfaction of a man who has accomplished his task and performed a good and meritorious work.

Preface

FOR many years my children, countless old friends and associates have frequently urged me to write a history of my early life. I hesitated for a long time to comply with these requests, thinking that I had experienced little that could be of any special interest to anybody except myself; but as I have witnessed the rapid growth of Texas in population during the past ten years with the many radical economic changes, I have many times compared the present times with those just after the Civil War; and I realized with astonishment that I was surrounded by a new world which had forgotten during the comparatively short space of one generation those times that marked, as it were, the infancy of our beloved Texas.

Many times I brought up in conversation with old friends reminiscences of times long past and heard the younger generation ask wonderingly why they had never heard or read of such conditions and circumstances as we, the older people, had met with. And I then decided to set down at least a short account of those times and exploits in which I had been for the past fifty-five years either spectator or actor.

It is, however, a rather precarious task for a pioneer to engage in writing. Those dear people who passed their youth with me in Texas are likewise as far from being authors as I confess to be, and I feel in the attitude of a man of letters or literature as awkward and uncomfortable as if I were obliged to ride my old cow pony, dressed in a frock-coat and stovepipe hat.

What I set down here are facts, witnessed or experienced by myself and faithfully preserved by a retentive memory.

Now that the old times have gone forever, I trust that my readers will peruse with more than passing interest the description of the primitive conditions which the forefathers had to contend with to prepare the soil and make life easier and more enjoyable for their descendants of the present day. If I can be instrumental in inducing our young people to love nature with its myriad charms and to feel confident that in this, our blessed country, no man need be afraid of failure if he with manly courage, perseverance, and honesty tries to do his best, I shall consider myself amply rewarded.

To Texas

THE winter of 1868 was a severe one, giving way slowly, almost imperceptibly, to the approaching springtime. I was among the many who suffered the hardest from the rigors of winter and who missed the best of all earthly possessions—sound health. When very young I contracted a slight affection of the lungs because of the cold climate of northern Germany, and being without the necessary means I was unable to follow the advice of my physician to pass some time in a southern and more congenial climate. My good mother, who was left poorly provided for by the early death of my father, worked with untiring zeal for the support of her children, and I, her youngest, was especially fortunate in acquiring an education. At the age of fourteen I was apprenticed to a silk-house in Berlin, and ever since that time I had to depend on my own efforts for a livelihood.

My salary was just enough to save me from starvation. I had to sleep in a garret and share my quarters with another young man. I therefore mused long and often how I was to shape my life in the days to come. I had no doubt that it was to be short, miserable, and full of privations because day by day I witnessed similar conditions among the people with whom I was brought in contact. But I clung to life with all the fibres of my being. I longed to start out in the world, to make my own way, and to become sound and well and able to enjoy the good things of this earth. I felt sure that the first step toward the realization of these wishes was a speedy recovery of my health, and to succeed in that I had to find my way to a milder climate. I conceived the plan to travel in France, the climate in the southern part being regarded as ideal for people suffering with diseases of the lungs.

One Sunday morning I was reading the *Berliner Intelligenzblatt* when I discovered an advertisement wanting a young man to serve as companion and interpreter for a family during the Exposition at Le Havre. I applied for the position and secured it, as I had mastered the French language fairly well. I had studied French at the Berlin High School, and my position in the silk-house afforded splendid opportunities to improve it by constant association and contact with young Frenchmen. On our way to Le Havre we met with little that was of special interest, and small indeed were the sympathies extended by the family I had to accompany, but the Exposition with its many and varied sights afforded me all the more pleasure. The weather was disagreeable throughout the two weeks we were away. It rained continually and in the chill and moisture of those days I contracted a severe cold that again affected my weak lungs. As it was useless to return to Germany, I resolved after short deliberation to travel on to Spain, expecting to find in this country the warm sunshine I was longing for. With twenty Prussian thalers and a small satchel in my possession I landed at Santander. I found the place bathed in the brightest sunshine, a condition which instantly revived my drooping spirits, and on the following day I tried to find employment. This was more difficult than I had imagined because I was really too weak for hard labor, while light work was poorly paid. Then, too, I only understood a few words of Spanish. After a few weeks my meager means were exhausted and the cold winds along the Bay of Biscay threatened to retard rather than promote my health. Consequently, I decided to emigrate to the island of Cuba, which at that time was in the throes of a revolution. The Spanish government was just sending a regiment of soldiers to Havana to quell the insurrection and had chartered for this purpose the small transport *Saxonia*, a Hamburg steamer.

A kind German resident of Santander procured for me permission of the Spanish officer to cross the ocean on this steamer provided I was willing to work for my passage and participate in the daily military exercises during my leisure hours. Arriving in Havana I was free to enter the ranks in case I was satisfied with the life of a soldier. The *Saxonia* was a small vessel of about 3,500 tons, and the entire regiment of eight hundred soldiers was embarked on it. My passage on board this steamer was one of the most unhappy experiences of my life; even now I think of it with disgust and aversion. There was hardly room for so many soldiers, and the filth brought on board by these people beggars description. The upper deck, reserved for military practices, could be kept tolerably clean, but the lower holds of the vessel fairly reeked with filth and vermin, for these soldiers had been recruited from the lowest classes of the Spanish population, and filth and dirt seemed to be their natural element. Our passage lasted three weeks, and as it was exceedingly stormy almost every person aboard was down with seasickness. We finally reached Cuba and the sight of the far-off shore fringed with clusters of graceful palm trees reconciled me somewhat to the terrors just passed. At a distance of half a mile from the shore the *Saxonia* cast anchor. Nobody was allowed to leave the vessel. A little later some officers came on board, ordering the ship to continue the journey the next morning and to sail to Santiago, where these fresh forces were needed for the military operations in progress. I was refused permission to leave the vessel, but the third mate took pity on me and promised to hire a small boat so I could secretly pass over to Havana after midnight.

Opportunities for effecting this plan were not wanting. Numerous small boats loaded with tropical products continually thronged around the steamer to sell their fruit to the sick and half-starved soldiers. About two o'clock one morning I made good my escape by sliding down a rope to the boat. I had to abandon my little trunk after I had taken out a few of the most important pieces of clothing, which I took along in a sack. My finances had now dwindled to a few dollars, but I felt happy nevertheless in my newly gained freedom because I could breathe the balmy air I had yearned for so long, and I resolved to celebrate this event by a feast even if I had to spend my last cent. Accordingly I rented a room with bath at a first-class hotel, and after I had cleaned up thoroughly and visited a barber, I partook of a breakfast such I had not enjoyed since my departure from Le Havre.

I later inspected Havana, a great city full of interesting sights for newcomers from Europe. Slavery still prevailed all over Cuba, and with sympathy and pity I looked at the half-naked, swarthy unfortunates who were daily sold or exchanged like cattle on the public slave market. At the same time I was impressed by the excessive luxury displayed by so many of the rich Cuban families. Every afternoon I could witness the so-called Corso, a pompous parade where the rich held a great celebration, at which many beautiful and fiery horses were exhibited hitched to carriages resplendent with silver plating or silver ornaments, and where richly dressed Cuban beauties bombarded the coaches of their passing friends with bouquets of flowers, while the gentlemen accompanied the carriages of their ladies mounted on the finest steeds. Add to this picture the splendid plazas with their groups of palms and beds of the most beautiful tropical flowers. But the most lively activity developed after sunset when real merrymaking began. During the excessive heat of the day most of the larger stores and residences of the capital were closed. After sunset, however, the streets swarmed with merry people enjoying the cool breezes and listening to the sweet tunes of the grand concerts given free in the gardens surrounding the government buildings, while the many luxurious drinking places resounded with the noise of the gay crowds.

During this, my first day in the city of Havana, my courage had grown by degrees, and I resolved to pay my bill, which I was sure would exhaust my finances, and to look out for a job in real earnest. But the next day when I asked for my bill, I was astonished to hear that everything had been settled, nor could I find out the name of my benefactor. I was of course curious to solve this riddle as well as pleased to stay another day at the hotel. I made good use of my powers of observation and watched closely the guests who were dining with me. Presently I discovered several gentlemen in one of the corners of the dining room smiling and looking in my direction. I went boldly to their table and asked them if they had been so generous as to settle my bill. Immediately they introduced themselves and I was surprised to find that the most considerate member of the party was the American consul for Cuba. They explained to me that it was a custom of theirs during the revolution to treat all newcomers as their guests and I was invited to share their hospitality for some time longer. Although their explanation did not appear very plausible, I accepted the consul's invitation with pleasure. I moved to his residence, and while I had no reason to be ashamed of my clothes,

I experienced considerable embarrassment for having to enter his home with a sack purloined from the *Saxonia*. Later over a glass of wine I told him how I had succeeded in slipping away from the boat. He was greatly amused by my story, for his secret sympathies were with the insurgents. I spent several days in his company visiting the sugar and tobacco plantations of the neighborhood, where half-naked darkies worked under the supervision of overseers who made frequent use of their whips. My last day with the consul was the most interesting. Early in the morning we sailed in his yacht to Moro Castle, the fortress which protected the entrance to Havana harbor. The flat coast stretching before our eyes was formed of stalactites. In many places the clear, blue water of the sea had washed out cavities or cul-de-sacs, and the receding flood had left pools of water. In one of the pools thus formed we enjoyed a swim, after which we partook of a substantial lunch and bottle of fine wine. We later sailed along the coast, which was thickly dotted with a great many beautiful shells, sea anemones, and many-colored corals, and I could not resist the temptation to take some of these beautiful specimens along with me.

After an hour's rest in the shade of a tall palm tree we penetrated a dense thicket full of large tropical flowers, descended the rock on which the fortress stands, and returned to our boat, which brought us safely back to Havana at sunset.

During this trip I conversed with the consul about my plans and prospects, and he gave a description of the conditions prevailing in Cuba that fully convinced me that it would be futile and useless to remain longer on the island. He later told me a great many things about the United States and its bright prospects and advised me to embark for New Orleans on board of one of the many steamers in the harbor. My means, however, were too slight for a three-day passage on any of them; besides, I did not wish to enter the land of liberty with empty pockets. The next morning I hired out to a small steamer bound for New Orleans as stoker in return for my passage and thus paid my way to the beautiful and interesting metropolis where I first set my foot on American soil.

I was now far from my native land and had seen enough of the world to contract a well-developed case of homesickness, but I soon recovered, realizing that my fortune, like that of most other emigrants, could not be improved by looking backward but only by looking forward, and that all my energies belonged to my newly adopted country.

I may state here without fear of contradiction that no nation in the wide world is subject to such an intense longing for travel as the German people. And along with this desire for adventure is their urge for work. No nation, moreover, enjoys and understands music as the Germans do, and the yearning for the Fatherland never dies out in the heart of the German immigrant. There is neither doctor nor medicine for this state of mind and many a poor fellow has had to succumb to it.

What is it that causes these sentimental longings? It is the German *soul*, that something that is denied other races and seldom understood by them.

For the German child fairies peep from every flower; eerie dwarfs people the mountains and supernatural beings flit through the woods. The German child believes these fairy tales, and where else in the world is life pictured happier and more beautiful than in a German fairy tale? The older people remember the charm of the ineffable German springtime with its flowers and singing birds and their ramblings through the German forests. They recall memories of friendships made during the school days and kept sacred throughout their lives. They compare the Christmas under the cedar tree with the joy found around the fir tree in the old country. They remember with loving secrecy how every preparation for the event was made and what a source of joy for them was the impatient expectation of their children! And, then, Christmas Eve, with its bright wax candles and its ever beautiful song of "Silent Night, Holy Night." How gratefully was each small gift received and cherished! This and much more was indelibly imprinted in our hearts and no power on earth can blot it out.

Yes, the Germans have given to the New World the Christmas tree, but the most precious gift—that sublime Christmas joy—they have kept to themselves. Such were the thoughts that surged through my mind when I entered the New World.

Deeply impressed as I was at Havana by its wealth of tropical vegetation, the excessive luxury of the European colony, and the abject slavery on the Cuban plantations with their poor, partly clad, and flogged Negroes, at New Orleans I was even more struck with the grandeur of the sights and scenes that met my eye on every side and the multitude and variety of peoples and races that commingled within its limits. But I found the city torn by party, racial, and political strife. This being immediately after the Civil War, the different parties and factions were bitterly opposed to each other.

The objects of the greatest detestation on the part of southerners were the so-called carpetbaggers, who came from the North carrying their earthly belongings in a carpetbag. They managed to obtain all the public offices, distributing them among themselves and their friends, while the vanquished southern population was disfranchised. The emancipated Negroes now demanded the right of suffrage, and feeling secure in superior numbers acted accordingly. Shooting and killing never stopped, and the approaching campaign for the presidential election only added fuel to the raging flames. General Grant was the northern candidate for the presidency, and we moderns of today have no conception of the bitterness that was engendered and prevailed between the two contending parties.

Meanwhile I had procured employment in a jewelry store, the owner of which has a claim to my lasting gratitude for assisting me in adapting myself to my new surroundings and circumstances. However, I held this position only two weeks, because in spite of all the new and interesting things that were transpiring in New Orleans, I longed to leave the city and get a glimpse of the Wild West. Like many other boys I had read Cooper's *Leatherstocking Tales* and similar Indian stories which represented their red-skinned heroes as brave and chivalrous warriors. Those stories and the romance of a life in the wilderness had an alluring influence upon my fancy, and when I read in the New Orleans *Deutsche Zeitung* a description of the atrocities perpetrated by the Comanches and Apaches on and among the Texas settlers, I was fully determined to start for Texas to brave the dangers of the wild Texas border life and see for myself what it actually was.

I again paid my passage working as a stoker on board a little steamer bound from New Orleans to Texas, and in the fall of 1868 I landed at the little port of Indianola on the Gulf of Mexico. Like all ports along the Gulf coast this town was built on the level, sandy sea coast. It was surrounded by lagoons which were the breeding places of millions of mosquitoes, tormenting man and beast with such fiendish pertinacity that it was impossible to get any sleep without the protection of mosquito-bars.

Indianola had the appearance of quite an active trading place, *being the center from where the entire commerce was handled to supply New Mexico, West Texas, and a large portion of Mexico along the Rio Grande and far into the interior.* The streets were alive with the teams freighting goods into the interior. *The large wagons drawn by six to twelve mules, called "prairie schooners," and the two-wheeled Mexican carretas, drawn by six to ten yoke of oxen, hauled their freight as far as El Paso, Texas, Santa Fe, New Mexico, and Chihuahua, Mexico. The many small forts established by the United States government were also supplied from this source. The life in Indianola appealed to me, the flower-covered prairies, the blue Gulf, the grotesquely clothed cowboys on their fiery Spanish ponies, and, more than all, the arsenal of arms each rider carried with him, and I made up my mind to remain for a time.*

The best hotel in the town belonged to a Mrs. Seider, commonly referred to as Mother Seider. During the first two days of my stay at Indianola I earned my living by catching fish, but on the third day a better opportunity presented itself. A steamer on the Morgan Line arrived with a cargo of two thousand barrels of flour which had to be discharged within a few hours. I was one of those who applied for work, the wages being one dollar an hour. Loading facilities such as are in general use today were unknown at the time. The barrels had to be rolled up by main force from the lower deck of the vessel to the higher landing bridge. I was the only white man in a crowd of thirty darkies, as I did not know then that work of this kind was done by Negroes almost exclusively, and the white people looking on at the landing laughed and made fun of me, and this induced the Negroes to resort to all kinds of tricks to make me disgusted with the work. I labored hard, as each one of these barrels weighed two hundred pounds, and I had to employ all my strength to roll them up the steep plank, while this was child's play for the robust Negroes. But they soon succeeded in their scheme, the particular darky working behind me watching every chance to roll his barrel against my heels, causing many painful bruises. I soon discovered what they were up to and amidst the laughter of spectators was forced to quit work, for which I did not receive any pay, as I left the job before the required number of hours terminated.

I next engaged in digging wells, and this might require some explanation. For drinking purposes the people used the water that ran down from the roofs and was caught in cypress cisterns. For all other purposes the rainwater that seeped through the soil and formed in small pools or wells was used. These shallow holes had a depth of about five feet and were of the same diameter.

For a week I was employed in this way when another small steamer entered the port, flying the English flag. It had a cargo of machines and boilers which were to be installed in a packing plant, the first of its kind in Texas. The principal part of the entire equipment consisted of a great upright steam boiler, twenty feet long and eight feet in diameter. When, after many difficulties, the boiler had been placed upon two large wagons to be transported across the dunes, the carrying capacity of the same was not equal to the enormous weight of the load, and at every pull of the teams the wheels would sink up to the axles. For two days the owners, Messrs. Ewell and Papin, tried in vain to get the boiler to the site where the plant was to be located, a distance of four miles. I was one of the curious crowd that watched their efforts. Suddenly an idea struck me how to move the boiler easily. I contracted with the proprietors to deliver it at its destination within half a day for one hundred dollars. At first they laughed at my suggestion and attempted to ascertain my plans, but I was not their dupe in this emergency, so in the evening they accepted my offer, and on the following morning I began my preparations. I had the boiler taken from the wagon and deposited in the sand. Long ox-chains were fastened to the two bars of the boiler and kept apart by means of a beam so as not to interfere with the motion of the boiler. The yoke of oxen was hitched to the chains and the heavy boiler rolled easily to the plant within three hours. I received my one hundred dollars and immediately accepted an offer of the owners to assist in installing the machinery.

I worked in this plant for several months, or until I could save enough money to purchase a *regular cowboy's outfit, consisting of a good horse, saddle, bridle, two large revolvers, a Spencer gun, and a blanket to sleep on.*

Early Experiences in Texas

DURING the Civil War most of the men had entered the southern armies, and those who were able to return after four years of service were so demoralized that they were unwilling to do any regular work. The women and children were obliged to look after themselves in many instances. The Federals had closed the Confederate states to commerce, as it were, and a strict embargo left the South destitute of almost every article of use. The North was the manufacturing center while the South had no factories at all. The women had to work in the fields to raise the corn necessary for their bread. There was a scarcity of meat because the cattle could not conveniently be brought to market. The old spinning wheels and looms —long discarded and stored away in obscure corners—were re-installed and sheep and cotton raised to supply the garments most needed. Thus it happened that for many years nobody cared for the rapidly increasing herds of wild cattle which in 1868 amounted to several million head. The price of one or two dollars a head paid then in Indianola actually amounted to no more than the wages of the drover. In the slaughter house where I was then working we al·ways kept a stock of about five hundred head. At night the beeves were kept in an enclosure made of boards and posts shipped from Florida, but during the day two cowboys would watch the cattle in the pastures. Having my own horse, I was now able to take the place of one of the cowboys, and it was here that I first acquired the art of horseback riding. I paid for it with many a bad fall, yet I have never ceased to like that kind of sport.

Whatever is connected with the occupation of a Texas cowboy

is peculiar to itself. He sleeps wrapped in his blanket near the enclosure or pen where the herd rests at night, but unfortunately the cattle do not remain quiet long. They are easily excited and move around incessantly. Sometimes a sudden fright seizes them on account of some trifling occurrence, and, mad with terror, all the animals plunge headlong in the same direction. This is known as a stampede. By the impact of their heavy bodies any part of a fence lying in the direction of their flight is torn down and the animals scatter to the four winds. The cowboy, ever alert even in sleep, hears the noise. He rushes to the spot where the cattle attempt to break through, and with heavy blows tries to repulse the wild creatures. Posts, fences, and other parts of the corral laid low during the stampede have to be repaired immediately. Sometimes it has been known where the cowboys succeeded in quieting the herd by singing, and long experience has taught him that certain melodies tend to appease the excited beasts. Strange to say, the first measures of Gungl's "Sounds of Home" were the favorite lullabies used by the cowboys, and they generally had the desired effect.

While we watched our herds, little sleep came to our eyes. At five o'clock in the morning we cooked our simple breakfast over a scanty fire. It was invariably the same: bread made of cornmeal, water, and salt and baked in a skillet, the tight-fitting lid of which was covered with live coals. Coffee was prepared in a tin can and very strong, and we drank it from tin cups without milk or sugar. There were slices of fried bacon, the hot grease remaining in the frying pan after the bacon had been removed and mixed with molasses. This kind of fare made up our breakfast, dinner, and supper. We never tired of it and remained sound and healthy.

At night, on his return to the camp, many tasks awaited the cowboy. Nearly every one of them was skilled in the making of all kinds of useful articles from rawhide. The hide was sliced into small straps or strips one-fourth to one-half of an inch wide, and when the hair had been shaved the strap hides were soaked in water and made soft and pliant. The first article every cowboy made was his short riding quirt, plaited from straps of rawhide. The quirt handle was made of a piece of iron rod and filled with lead to serve as a weapon in case of necessity. Everything made of rawhide was practically indestructible. An article of especial pride was the lasso, a long strap of rawhide about forty feet long and five-eighths of an inch in diameter, at the loop-end of which was fastened a small iron ring that served to close the noose easily when the rope alighted on the animal and held it securely by the horns. The hobble was another necessary article in a cowboy's outfit. It was strapped around the forefeet of the grazing horses to prevent them from moving too far from camp or headquarters, and so they could be caught more easily. Also the saddle had to be supplied with many straps, so the movable property of the owner, such as raincoat and shirts, could be fastened to it. The log-cabin chairs and mattress rests were made of rawhide; and with the same material the ox teams were tied to our Mexican carts directly by the horns. These carts were supplied with two very high and thick wheels. Many a time when they happened to lose their tires we bound them with wet rawhides, which, when dry, contracted and served their purpose nearly as well as iron hoops, particularly as long as the dry weather lasted. But the crowning achievement of the Texas cowboy's possessions was his saddle—Texas made. Different in shape from all other kinds of saddles in the world, it sometimes weighed as much as fifty pounds. The saddletree proper was made of tough wood; its high pommel in front had to be wrought of the fork of a tree. Re-inforced by screws and bolts, the tree was then entirely covered with rawhide. Heavy pieces of leather protected the legs of the rider; the stirrup covers had to be eight inches wide and the stirrups themselves so wide as to cover the entire foot. To the saddle horn the lasso is fastened, and it must be strong enough to throw the strongest bull at full speed with a single jerk. An indispensable part, moreover, of every cowboy's equipment is a pair of strong, leather breeches, or leggings. They cover the body from the belt to the soles of the feet. Their inside, touching the body, is lined with soft pliable leather; the outside is of heavy sole leather. The leggings answer many purposes—but above all they protect the cowboy's clothing when he is galloping through underbrush and high, thorny cactus plants. They also afford protection against mad bulls, the horns of which are ever ready to gore the horses as well as the legs and bodies of the cowboys, and last but not least they are of excellent use when untamed, vicious, and bucking horses are being broken, since the cowboy's legs weighted down with these leggings, or "chaps," are not so apt to lose their hold at every jump of the horse. But the most important item of a cowboy's outfit of course is the horse itself.

Before the year 1870 most of the animals in Texas were the off-spring of horses left by Spanish conquerors (conquistadores) in Mexico and Texas. These horses or broncos were short and stout, with well-formed head, intelligent eyes, and long mane and tail nearly touching the ground. Their hooves were so tough that it was seldom necessary to shoe them, and their endurance was never equalled by any other member of the equine tribe. In later years they were crossed with native or American sires, especially of the Morgan breed, and in many instances Arabian stallions were imported for breeding purposes. But for herding cattle the Spanish ponies were best suited, and it was on such an animal that I made my first trip into the interior of Texas.

My First Visit to Victoria

I remained at Indianola longer than I intended, owing to an epidemic of yellow fever. At that time there was no known cure for this dread disease. Large doses of quinine were used but to no avail, for after the usual black vomiting the patients generally succumbed within a few days, sometimes within a few hours. A young German, Frank Boehm, who had also been employed by my boss, was a victim of this fatal malady. Boehm was a good, simple soul but so tenderhearted that he could never overcome his homesickness. He had studied forestry at Altenburg, Saxony, and had immigrated to America without ever being able to find congenial employment. Being the only German in the camp besides myself, he naturally sought my company and soon we were inseparable friends. One night while sharing my pallet with me he was attacked by yellow fever. We had neither doctors nor nurses so I nursed him myself and never left his bedside until on the third day he expired in my arms. I mourned for him as if he had been my own brother. Among his few belongings I found some letters with the addresses of his relatives which enabled me to communicate to them the sad news of his untimely death.

I was free now to leave Indianola and start northward, and I never saw the dear old town again. In the eighties of the last century an enormous spring tide washed the entire city into the Gulf, and it was never rebuilt. No picture can give a true idea of the destruction wrought by our beautiful Gulf within a few hours, when its breakers, lashed to a height of from fifteen to twenty feet by West Indian hurricanes, surge over the sands of the low Texas coast.

My first destination was the little town of Victoria, which I could barely reach in a day and a half; therefore I did not leave Indianola until noon, intending to camp out in the open air the first night.

There were no barbed wire fences in those days, nor were there any trees from which to make fences or enclosures. The boundless prairie, covered with many-colored wildflowers and teeming with prairie chickens, extinct long ago, wild rabbits, herds of deer, and thousands of wild cattle, stretched before my eyes, while human beings and habitations were scarce and far between.

Looking down upon the prairie from on horseback my eyes met an endless variety of wildflowers—pink, red, purple, violet, blue, and yellow—and since most of them grew in clusters, this wide flowery expanse looked from afar like a veritable Turkish rug, and my horse's legs wading through these flowery masses were dyed a bright yellow by their golden pollen up to his knees. It would be a difficult task indeed to describe all of Flora's wild children, but I cannot refrain from describing at least five of the brightest, especially the wild phlox. This flower with its serrated leaves, growing ten or more inches high, bears on its stem a cluster of eight to ten starlike, velvety blossoms, the petals of which shine forth in a wonderfully brilliant blood red, surpassing even the beautiful tints of the rose. When cultivated the graceful little plant develops a variety of other tints ranging from white to violet, but none can equal the brilliancy of the wildflower's blood red.

The next flower worth mentioning is the bluebonnet, so called because from a distance it resembles a lady's sunbonnet. Somewhat larger than the phlox, it bears a pyramidal crown of delicate blossoms of a saturated cobalt blue and is so prolific that not only small patches but wide stretches of area and indeed entire prairies are covered with them. Some of the most beautiful pictures of Texas artists present landscapes adorned with a profusion of these lovely flowers.

Another attractive child of the Texas Flora is the buttercup, the white, pink, and yellow blossoms of which somewhat resemble those of the hedge-rose. It too grows in large clusters and possesses a very delicate fragrance, so it is difficult which to admire most, the beauty of the blossom or its delightful perfume.

And fourth but not least in importance is the goldenrod, one of the glories of the autumnal prairie, with its bright yellow flower heads which have given an entire prairie its name and form, in union with the flowers already named—a symphony of prodigious colors—a veritable paradise. The number and brilliance of hundreds of many-colored butterflies flitting through the balmy air and courting the flowers of the prairie I shall only mention without attempting to describe them. The fifth is the delicate plant called the touch-me-not, with its sweet-scented blossoms and serrated leaves which close at the slightest touch only to open again after ten or fifteen minutes.

One cannot dwell, however, continually under palms in perfect bliss, and even this paradise has its disadvantages and its pests. There is the botfly, the screw-worm fly, and the Texas tick. The botfly lays its eggs in the long hair of the horse. By scratching itself with its teeth, the horse transfers these eggs into its stomach, where they rapidly develop into worms which attack the walls of the stomach, causing serious fits which must be immediately and effectively attended to in order to save the animal. The horse instinctively knows its enemy and tries to flee from it by running away, or wards it off with hoof and tail, but is pursued by the insect with a demoniacal and unfortunately almost always successful pertinacity. The sensible horseman dismounts and rescues his horse by killing these pests, which is easily done as the insect is so intent on laying its eggs that it neglects all caution.

Then there is the tick—this ugly parasite, not any larger than a lentil, is a native of Texas and a curse and an abomination to every livestock breeder. It is to be found on grass blades, leaves, tree trunks, in fact, everywhere, and it infests dogs, cattle, horses, sheep, and other livestock which happen to touch the insect's hiding place. These ubiquitous pests, which multiply by the thousands, crawl into the ears and secrete themselves on other parts of the body where the infected animal cannot remove them, burying their heads deep into the animal tissue drawing the lifeblood of their victims. While the head is embedded in the flesh of the victim, the remainder of its body grows to three times its normal size and assumes an ugly gray color. By draining the blood and vitality of cattle and horses tick fever is superinduced, an infectious disease similar to tuberculosis develops, and the animal soon dies. When the tick has sucked sufficient blood or nourishment for its eggs, it drops to the ground to breed and leaves a bleeding wound on the released animal. And next the gadfly comes in, depositing its eggs around and near the bleeding wound. These eggs hatch in from three to thirty-six hours, with the result that small maggots soon bury themselves in the living flesh, causing ugly, deep-running channels into the vital parts and killing or crippling the tortured animal. Of late years the federal and state governments have taken in hand the matter of exterminating the tick and gadfly, which annually cause heavy losses to the livestock industry as well as endless torture to helpless animals.

A short description of that country which I had traversed on horseback may not be out of place here. With a kind of proud complacency I chased rabbits, forced my horse into all sorts of gaits, dreamed of adventures, and built aircastles for the days to come. Only a few hours were necessary for me to bring myself to a full realization of the stern truths of life. When the sun was nearing the horizon I dismounted, hobbled my horse, and turned him loose to feast on the fine grass. I made my coffee in a tin can and partook of a simple supper and went to sleep on the luxurious grass. Several hours later I was aroused from my dreams by heavy peals of thunder, and rising immediately, I beheld incessant flashes of lightning playing over the sky and witnessed an electrical storm of indescribable grandeur and such as can only be seen in a subtropical climate. The rain began to come down in torrents, and as everything in Texas runs to extremes, this rain was no exception. The watercourses and streams rose rapidly and inundated all the surrounding valleys. Anything that happened to be in the way of the destructive torrent was washed away.

I had been so inconsiderate, or thoughtless, I should say, as to camp out in a sharp depression of the land, so that the flood covered my saddle and I had to stand in the water until daybreak because in the dark I could not even find my horse or any place of refuge. But at dawn I was able to find him and, wet to the skin, I traveled on. The rain continued for two days. The black soil of the prairie was so boggy that my horse was barely able to travel. On the third day I reached the Guadalupe River, and just beyond it I saw the town of Victoria.

The river had risen more than fifty feet during the night and had washed the ferry boat away. I met a half-dozen people from various places on the river bank who were in the same plight I was in. Since we had hardly any provisions and, according to the opinion of some of the more experienced fellow-sufferers, could not expect the river to fall for several days, we decided to construct a small raft and risk the passage. The river banks throughout Texas are thickly wooded, so, after finding two good axes in a deserted Negro hut, we soon felled a half-dozen trees whose trunks we tied together in the form of a raft with tough grapevines. At the weakest points we replaced the vines with our lassoes, and with incredible pains we dragged this product of our first efforts at shipbuilding half a mile up the stream, undressed, fastened our clothes on our saddles, and, taking a firm hold of the raft, left it to the mercy of the current. Our horses, led by our lassoes, were swimming to the rear of the raft. At our starting point the Guadalupe made a decided bend and we observed that the trend of the main current was toward the opposite bank. Upon this fact we based our calculation, for indeed about half a mile below the town the current carried us near the opposite bank from which we had set out. Our horses having covered a distance of about a mile by swimming now seemed to be on the verge of exhaustion, but they no sooner noticed the approaching bank than they instinctively renewed their efforts, and swimming as they now were in front of our raft, they helped us materially to effect a safe landing. Some of the inhabitants of the town who had witnessed our exertions received us hospitably, and after we had been provided with dry clothing, we soon recovered from our hardships.

My journey from Indianola to Victoria, a distance of about fifty miles, led me across one of the most extensive prairie regions in Texas, on which I could not discover a tree or even a bush. Near the Gulf I encountered only the coarse sage-grass, containing much salt and little nourishment; therefore, it is unfit for pasturage. But as I traveled small patches of a finer grass appeared, and sometimes even the excellent mesquite grass was in evidence, and though short it is not equalled in nourishment by any other kind of grass and sustains cattle even during the winter season. It is called mesquite grass because it can be found wherever the mesquite tree grows,

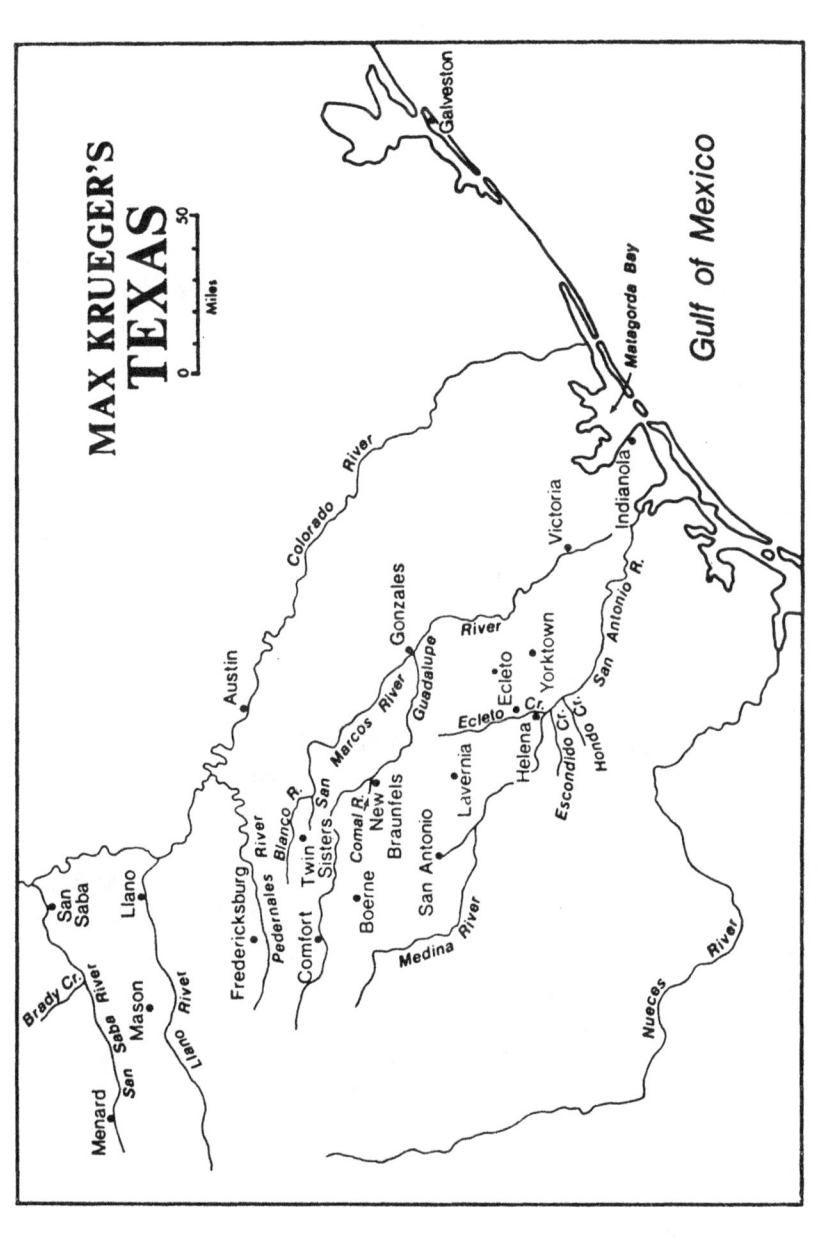

namely, in more than half of the entire state. It was a well-established belief in those days that the vast prairies along the Gulf were unfit for agriculture, but at the time this is written, this region —about fifty miles wide and more than five hundred miles long— represents one of the most intensively cultivated farming districts of all Texas. Besides extensive oil wells this plain possesses other subterranean riches. A few years ago when prospectors were drilling for oil they found at a depth of less than eight hundred feet immense deposits of sulfur, highly valuable and remarkably free of undesirable components. Large layers or deposits of sulfur are usually met with in the neighborhood of volcanoes, the most extensive being on the island of Sicily close by Mount Aetna, but great quantities are also found in the extinct craters near Mexico City.

Up to about twenty years ago sulfur was mined from deep pits by laborers, usually Italians, who loaded the sulfur into sacks and transported it to the surface on their backs, using only ladders. But an ingenious invention of a German engineer has replaced this primitive method and transferred the monopoly of the sulfur trade from the Old to the New World, leaving the mines in Sicily and other countries practically worthless. Basing his invention on the well-know fact that sulfur is easily liquified, the German inventor had two sets of great steam pipes sunk into the sulfur stratum. By the steam supplied through one pipe the sulfur was melted and forced to the surface along the other pipes by steam pressure. The liquid sulfur was then transferred to huge reservoirs where it cooled and immediately regained its original consistency. Much time and money were saved by directly stowing the sulfur in sea-going vessels. The sulfur deposits of Texas are so vast that all the world can be supplied with it for years to come.

The great streams and water routes of Texas have much in common. The Rio Grande, the boundary line between Texas and Mexico, rises outside of the state, as does the Red River, which separates Texas from Oklahoma. The remaining four principal rivers—the Nueces, Guadalupe, Colorado, and Brazos—rise in the northern part of Texas, while the sources of the San Antonio River gush forth near the city of the same name at a distance of 150 miles from the Gulf. All these rivers empty into the Gulf of Mexico and not one of them is navigable, because the quantity of their waters materially decreases during the summer months, while they are turned into destructive torrents by heavy showers of rain. They each have a strong fall and their waters passing through loose soil have left high and deeply cut banks. All the river valleys produce various kinds of valuable timber, the best specimen being, beyond any doubt, the pecan tree. Of all nuts it possesses the finest flavor. There are pecan trees ranging in diameter from two to five feet. The leaves of the pecan tree are oily and resemble those of the walnut tree. They afford a splendid shade and their wood is manufactured into many valuable kinds of furniture. Unfortunately only small quantities of this splendid nut are exported, as the people of North America appreciate their value and reserve them for home consumption.

Among the other kinds of trees to be found in the Texas river valleys I should like to mention the water elm and burr oak, fine straight trees of great dimensions, the wood of which, like that of the other kinds of oak, can be used for a variety of purposes.

Another valuable tree is the southern or Texas cypress, the red core of which supplies a wood that it almost immune to the ravages of time. It is used principally for cisterns, but alas! is becoming extinct, as the demand is greater than the supply and there are no laws or regulations affording it any protection. Extensive forests of pine and fir can be found only in the sandy parts of East Texas. The longleaf pine supplies excellent building material that is free of knots.

The mesquite tree belongs to a species of acacias. Its blossoms are a few inches long and very delicately shaped and sweet-scented. The beans developing from these blossoms are from four to six inches long and a favorite food for horses and cattle. When dried on the tree they keep for years, and up to the middle of the seventies of the last century they were gathered for food. Later on agriculture made rapid progress and corn was planted to take their place. The mesquite tree is specifically a Texas plant and is found on an area of more than fifty thousand square miles. The sweet resin frequently exuded by this tree was also gathered and used in place of gum arabic for pasting.

Texas Scenes

HAVING rested my horse for several days, I continued my trip into the interior. There was not, as far as I can remember, in 1868, a single bridge across the western rivers after the flood of that year. I had to go far out of my way to find a shallow place or ford. When crossing a deep river we cowboys used to push our horses from a high bank into the water and gain the opposite bank by holding on to their tails. Vehicles, generally drawn by six or eight yoke of oxen, had to wait on the banks until the water had receded. As there were neither highways nor even passable country roads in those days, it happened very often after a rain that the heavy wheels of the oxcart would sink into the mud up to the axles. We then had to wait till the ground was dry in order to continue our journey. I likewise made slow progress on my journey, but the change of scenery kept me interested throughout and reconciled me to my tardy advance. In place of the open prairie with its black soil I now encountered stretches of deep sand. Large tracts were covered with postoak trees and here and there a patch of blackjacks. These trees were seldom larger than two or three feet in diameter and never reached a height greater than thirty feet. They were used only for firewood by the settlers. Later, as these regions became more thickly settled, the trunks were split into fence rails and used to enclose the small fields so as to protect them from the wild cattle.

It was on these prairies that I first saw the chaparral bushes. They generally grew in dense clusters, forming compact thickets. During the long days of spring and summer the chaparral blossoms exhale an exceedingly sweet odor, and I know of no artificial perfume that can favorably compare with the fragrancy of those chaparral blossoms. For miles around they attract the bees, which come in swarms to reap a harvest of the sweetest honey, which commands an especially high price in the markets because it retains all the natural aroma of the blossoms.

The chaparral thickets are the favorite resort of thousands of rabbits. Here I also met with numerous flocks of Texas and Mexican partridges. But the most interesting feathered inhabitant of these parts was the tiny hummingbird, buzzing like a butterfly from flower to flower to drink in with its long bill the sweets contained in their cups. Here too I found for the first time the so-called bird-of-paradise. Its beautiful tail feathers adorn many a lady's hat of the present day. Wild pigeons, field larks, red cardinals, and bluebirds which are met with almost everywhere in Texas embellished and enlivened the scenery. But before I conclude my description of the sandy country which I traversed, I desire to call attention to the stately evergreen liveoak trees which are indigenous to those sections of the country. Their wood is almost as hard as iron; their trunks attain more than six feet in diameter and an age of from three to six hundred years, as the rings on the trees proved when I examined them. With their long and heavy branches they cover a space approximating a hundred feet square, enabling man as well as animals to enjoy their cool shade during the hot hours of the day. The comforts of this shade are made more enticing by the many mustang grapevines that generally creep up the trunks of liveoak trees and cover their tops with luxuriant foliage. The mustang vine seems to be of indestructible hardiness. Near the ground I frequently found these vines to be more than eight inches thick. The shade of the evergreen liveoak affords the grapevine protection from the scorching rays of the sun, while the sandy soil, permitting its roots to reach a considerable depth, enhances its fertility, so that each year the liveoaks are loaded down by a marvelous crop of wild grapes. Not even during my later travels through tropical countries, especially Brazil, which is famous for its grand forests, have I ever enjoyed a sight that would equal in beauty the one presented by those gigantic Texas oaks covered with the verdant canopy of the mustang vine.

The sky in this latitude is ever blue and serene; the tempera-

ture of the water permits of bathing even in winter, so the Gulf of
Mexico therefore could be called one of the ideal pleasure resorts
of the world. There are, however, many drawbacks. Many of the
bathers are afraid of the dolphins, large fish of the cetaceous tribe
that inhabit the Gulf waters in great numbers. But as a matter of
fact these graceful mammals are entirely harmless; however, the
sharks which show up now and then are by no means pleasant companions. There are, besides, a great many seastars (radiata) and
jellyfish swimming on the surface of the water. The latter have, as
their name would indicate, bodies of a soft, jelly-like consistency
and are very pretty indeed on account of their delicate hues, but
cause an unpleasant sensation not unlike the sting of the nettle.
Then there is a kind of flounder called stingaree that hides in the
sandy bed of the Gulf. Instead of the broad tail of the common variety, this flounder is provided with a snake-like organ from six
to eight inches long, which at its end has a stinger concealed, se-
creting a poisonous substance. When stepped upon this stinger
pierces the foot of the unsuspecting victim with its barbed hook,
generally causing permanent paralysis of the body and in extreme
cases gangrene and death. Fortunately the number of this dangerous species is limited. The tarpon or silver king yearly entices a
great many sportsmen to spend their summers on the Texas coast.
Its real home is the Mexican coast between Tampico and Veracruz.
It is generally met with in the shallow bayous and inlets leading
from the Gulf to the interior because these places teem with small
fish on which they feed. The silver king justly deserves its name, its
large scales glistening in the sunny waters like polished silver. The
tarpon grows to be more than six feet in length and weighs as much
as seventy-five to one hundred pounds, sometimes more. Catching
this giant of the Gulf waters is an exciting and interesting sport,
requiring a good boat and two men, one of whom has to keep the
boat moving at a moderate speed while the other has to watch the
fish that serves as bait. The hooks are not barbed but are fastened
to a line about three-eighths of an inch thick and one hundred feet
long, only thirty feet of which are cast into the water; the remaining seventy feet are wound around a reel and gradually let out when
the tarpon has swallowed the bait and tries to escape. Here the fun
begins. The tarpon offers a stubborn resistance, and the two fisher-

men seldom succeed in hoisting it into the boat until after several hours and then only after the tarpon's strength is completely exhausted. Many of the tarpon thus caught are stuffed and kept as souvenirs or trophies.

One more word about the coast. How different from the present time was its aspect in those days. The lagoons were covered with many thousands of wild geese and ducks which from their hatching places in the Canadian swamps migrated over two thousand miles to spend the winter on the warm coast of the Gulf of Mexico with its wealth of every kind of fish. Also probably more than half the pelicans in the United States have their permanent habitat on the Texas coast. But the most splendid spectacle is exhibited by that elegant bird called the flamingo, a kind of heron that is native to southern Mexico and comes to be our regular guest during the summer months. It is difficult to conceive anything more beautiful than the wonderful plumage of these birds displaying all the hues of the rainbow when they proudly stalk the shallow waters in search of frogs and small fish. Pure white, delicate pink, and various tints of light blue are the principal colors of its plumage.

The rivers on the Texas coast abound in fish. The catfish grow to weigh as much as sixty pounds and are only fairly good to eat. The freshwater eels also afford a repast for those who like them. The watercourses in the vicinity of the Gulf at one time contained many alligators, which were killed for their skins. Nowadays there is little need of hunting alligators, for their eggs are exposed to and hatched by the sun and the young creatures are carefully raised, as the value of their skins has greatly increased.

The most dangerous inhabitant of our rivers is the black moccasin, or water snake, the bite of which is nearly always fatal. This reptile can be avoided, however, as it cannot bite except on the surface of the water.

Of saltwater fish there are a multitude in the Gulf of Mexico. The bottom of the Gulf is covered for miles with oysters, the largest and most desirable being the Berwick Bay oyster. Redfish, a very palatable sort of fish, is indigenous to the Texas coast, and mackerels come swarming in incredibly large schools at certain seasons and are caught in nets. Another species is the splendid sea trout, glittering in a variety of colors, the spotted kind being the choicest. Many varieties of crawfish are also found along the Gulf, most of them edible. Some of them have a very lateral motion when on dry land. The catfish already referred to can live and thrive in salt water but according to my observation will not grow larger than about two pounds. It is a peculiarity of these fish to have their fins exceedingly stiff and full of a poison that will cause ulcers and even tetanus in many cases.

Helena

After a few days I rode on to Yorktown, where I hired to a farmer by the name of Carl Gerhardt. This was the time when the locust plague invaded Texas, and if the one through which the Egyptians went, according to the Bible, was similar, I feel sorry indeed for them. In a few weeks there was not a blade of grass left, the fields were empty, the trees were without leaves, and the wells and springs were covered a foot high so people could not drink the water. Even the curtains, bedclothes, and wearing apparel were devoured. After helping to clean a number of wells, I proceeded on my journey toward San Antonio. The many exposures I passed through brought about my old lung trouble, and when near Lavernia, I had a severe hemorrhage and became too weak to continue my travels. A kind old ranchman took care of me for a few days, and when able to mount a pony I took his advice and joined his cow camp on the Escondido and became a regular cowboy.

One evening two ranchmen coming from Mexico, where they had sold some American-bred stallions, stopped with us overnight. The one, Jack Scragens, whose children still live in Karnes County, spoke of a German by the name of Charley Brown, but whose real name was Krueger, whom he had met years ago in Brownsville and who now lived near Helena. Since we had our last letter from my brother dated at Brownsville, I had little doubt about his being my brother Carl, whom I had not seen for ten years and whom the family had heard from only three times during all this time. After two days' ride I found him in a log cabin near the San Antonio River, married to a soldier's widow by the name of Kennick. She was his

senior by several years, had two children, and had squatted on the
then free land of the state and tried to make a living by raising a
few horses.

Carl had been a soldier in the Confederate Army all during the
Civil War, and, having led a pretty wild life, partly in Mexico, was
entirely Americanized and very different from the picture I had in
mind. We soon agreed to disagree and I rode over to Helena to find
work.

Arriving at Helena from Victoria in December, 1868, I decided
to remain there for some time, and being among native Americans
I had a far better chance to get in touch with the life then in vogue
after the Civil War than at the towns of Victoria, Indianola, or Clinton with their mixed population. A largely German population recruited from the revolutionists of 1848 had settled in these communities. Of a total of about 300,000 inhabitants which Texas
claimed in the sixties, many of them had emigrated from all parts
of the globe, but the different nationalities generally confined their
intercourse to members of their own race, so it came to pass that
German settlements such as New Braunfels and Fredericksburg
preserved their German characteristics, and as the medium of communication was the German language, the newcomer felt as much
at home in "New Germany" as in the Fatherland.

Aside from these honest German farmers, a part of the population of Texas consisted of the human scum and refuse of all the
states of the Union. Those who were on bad terms with the law
sought and found a hiding place in Texas, and the reputation of our
state did not profit by this fact.

The town of Helena had two hotels, four saloons, a blacksmith
shop, a drug store, and a half-dozen business houses where most of
the necessities could be bought. About forty primitive residences,
consisting of frame houses and rude log cabins scattered over a
space of several miles, gave shelter to a total population of about
three hundred souls. Besides the regular occupation of cattle driv-
ing a favorite pastime of these people was stealing horses. Some of
the menfolk, provided they were not idling their time away in the
whiskey dens and adjoining gambling resorts, were constantly on
their way to Mexico, a distance of 150 miles, to exchange the American stallions purloined in North and East Texas for Mexican ponies,

these ponies in turn being sold in those parts of East Texas that had been thrown open for immigration.

Another favorite sport of the natives was looting the great freight wagons carrying goods from Indianola to San Antonio, Concho, and other military posts. As there was no beer to be had at that time, whiskey was consumed in great quantities, so that the smallest trifles frequently led to quarrels which were settled with the six-shooter or Bowie knife. Here originated that murderous atrocity called after the town itself—the "Helena duel." The manner of fighting it out was this: the left hands of the two combatants were tied together with deerskin straps and their right hands provided with pocket knives, the blades of which were no more than three inches long. They were then given several rapid turns, after which they were told to begin and were not allowed to stop until one of the party had bled to death. A large part of the inhabitants used to surround the duelists and watch eagerly the progress of the fight. The pocket knives used for this bloody massacre were purposely kept short so as to prevent the opponents from striking the heart or some other vital part. This arrangement also served the added purpose of prolonging the cruel spectacle for the amusement of the assembled crowd.

As a matter of course horses were the most valuable and necessary property, as there were neither highways nor railroads at the time; consequently horse-stealing was in full swing, despite the fact that every horse thief who was caught was promptly hanged by the "vigilantes," a kind of secret court which existed throughout the West in the pioneer days. Unfortunately, some innocent person who had been falsely accused on account of envy or for some other reason was sometimes hanged. A murder was never punished in Helena, but there were feuds whenever a reason for them could be found. The authorities had no power to check this lawlessness, and many officers who tried to do their sworn duty were themselves killed. No man left his home without being heavily armed, the principal weapons being the same as those used in the Civil War: the Spencer carbine, Colt's forty-four six-shooter, which had to be loaded with powder and ball, and the long, heavy Enfield rifles converted into short guns.

When I went to Helena an old settler by the name of Monroe

Shots invited me to pass a few days with him on Hondo Creek. My attentions were equally divided between my host and his neighbors, Jack Scragens and John Paschal. These were troublesome times for the Helena people, as the arrival of military forces threatened to curtail the wild and unrestrained habits of certain undesirable citizens. *When one day five peaceful Poles who came to Helena to do some trading were put up as targets and killed in cold blood, the United States Government located two companies of cavalry in the town to establish peace and order.*[1]

Being a stranger, I of course was not allowed to attend the secret nightly meetings of the local citizens, but I was well aware that some mischief was brewing. On the fourth night of my stay a large detachment of heavily armed soldiers arrived in Helena, continuing their march until after midnight. The next morning I heard what had happened. A troop of soldiers had been ordered to arrest some of the people who had declared themselves. These were hiding at a ranch on Escondido Creek, and to arrest them the soldiers had to cross Hondo Creek. It had been decided at the secret meeting to ambush the soldiers at the crossing in order to prevent them from further interference with the affairs of the community. There was a deep layer of fine sand at the bottom of the river which was turned into a soft mass by heavy rains, forming the so-called quicksand. As the soldiers were ignorant of this condition, horses and riders sank deep into the sand and, unable to reach the opposite bank, were entirely helpless. At this unpropitious juncture the soldiers were attacked. The river was swollen by the rains of the preceding days and this aided the assailants materially. Several soldiers were killed and many of the settlers wounded. For the capture, dead or alive, of one of them, Fred Hannon, the government had offered a reward. This man, having been shot in the thigh and severely wounded, had been concealed in a dense cactus thicket. In consequence of this attack the military measures became more stringent. Large detachments of soldiers searched the surrounding ranches and it was dangerous for people to leave their homes. For a week I was forced to care for this wounded man, and regularly after mid-

[1] For other sufferings of the Poles of Panna Maria at the hands of their neighbors, see Hedwig Krell Didear, *A History of Karnes County and Old Helena* (Austin: San Felipe Press, 1969), pp. 22–44.

night I rode to his hiding place, eight miles distant, washed and dressed his wounds, and refreshed him with food and water; it was here that I learned to appreciate the marvelous healing powers of the cactus leaves. A little later at Helena I learned that Fred Hannon was able to mount his horse just a month after receiving his wound and that he had left the country never to return.

I had intended to earn my living as a cowboy, but as herding and corralling the cattle did not begin until springtime, I was forced to consider other means of livelihood, at least for the time being. *My first work here was the grinding of corn on the windmill built after the Dutch style. The surrounding squatters brought their grain on horseback to the mill, and during a night when a good stiff norther blew I could grind as much as eighty bushels. The toll was one-half for grinding, and this half was divided in equal parts between the owner and myself. However, the mill changed hands frequently, as it served as an admirable stake for gambling, and when one evening at eight o'clock I was informed that John Paschal had won the mill and at midnight John Ruckman was the new owner, I quit the job. By this time the United States government reached the conclusion that the two companies of soldiers would have their hands full for a year or more, and prepared to build a few frame warehouses to keep in store the provisions and horsefeed needed. I undertook to put up these buildings for a wage of one hundred dollars per month and rations, and had permission to use additional help at the same wages. As my brother Carl was in needy circumstances, I took him in as a partner, his wife doing the cooking for all of us.*

These warehouses were crude affairs, the material for their construction being delivered by oxcarts. They were to be built on the top of an adjoining hill to make for greater security, and as light conveyances were not available in those days, the entire material was literally dragged up the hill by hitching it to the tails of our horses, and the water used in the homes was dragged up by being fastened to the saddle pommel.

When our two warehouses were completed, I contracted the malaria fever, as it was called in those days, which laid me up for about four months. The only medicine we used were the red peppers which grew plentiful in the woods and the wild "camo," with a taste more bitter than quinine. Since ice was an unknown luxury and no lemon had ever reached us, you can imagine what patients suffered in those times during the fearful hot days without a cooling drink. When the fever was nearly broken my finances were also at an end, and I had to look again for employment. The Riedel brothers at Ecleto were building a sawmill, and I was employed to chop the large burr and postoaks down and haul the logs with ox teams to the mill. The rations were cornbread, molasses, bacon, and coffee, and the work lasted fourteen hours a day. We had to sleep on blankets in the prairie and the pay amounted to fifteen dollars per month. Of this I managed to save about five dollars a month for a rainy day. After the sawmill was completed, a corn mill and cotton gin were added, and also the first frame building went up for the Riedel family to live in.

Soon afterward, William Menn added a small country store to the little colony. Mrs. William Menn invited her sister Emily Buergener for a visit, and on Christmas Day, 1870, Emily and I were married. Emily was sixteen years old at that time and I had my nineteenth birthday two days after our wedding day.

How rosy the future looked at this age; it seemed as if life could hold nothing but sunshine for us, but it was not long until dark clouds gathered over our heads. Emily's relatives opposed our union very much, and it soon came to blows between me and my brothers-in-law, so I thought it best to go back into cowboy life. Collin Campbell of Ecleto prepared to take a large herd of cattle to Kansas, and I hired to him as one of the hands. Emily was to remain during my absence with her sister Christiana Menn. Each cowboy had to furnish two horses and received wages of $75 per month. The drive was to last four months and I expected to save $250 during this time. From this we expected to set up housekeeping. During the gathering of the herd of 1,500 head, I had the opportunity to visit Emily frequently, but it was a sad day when the hour of parting came. As happened so often in my life, I planned things beautifully, but not often have I been able to carry these plans to perfection. The herd was hard to handle, the grass was poor, and we had many stampedes which took the strength of our horses.

Cattle Country

IN those days the cattle business was vastly different from the cattle industry of the present. During the Civil War nobody cared for the thousands of cattle in Texas, and they were practically without owners and roamed at will over the vast expanses of grazing territory. Anybody not afraid of work could brand these animals by marking a letter or some symbol on the cattle by means of a red-hot branding iron, and an animal thus marked or branded was considered the property of the owner of the branding iron.

Many a man who had returned from the war with means was able to hire certain cowboys to brand these cattle for him, and since the cattle increased rapidly, a great many of the so-called cattle kings came on the scene with thousands of head in their possession. The great pastures were the property of the State of Texas and free to all. Land of the best quality was worthless because there was no market for it. Many large tracts were sold for as little as twenty-five cents an acre. Later, some who had not participated in this gigantic theft began to protest, seeing that many thousands of cattle had become the property of a few individuals who, in addition to acquiring their herds in the manner indicated, could also feed them on the public domain, yet taxes for the maintenance of the government were supposed to be imposed on all inhabitants alike.

When the situation or condition just described had reached the point where personal remonstrances were of no avail and the arguments proffered at the point of a six-shooter did not have the desired effect, a compromise was entered into permitting every Texan to claim wild cattle by simply branding them, but care had to be taken not to start his promiscuous branding before a certain day in the spring. Every person thus engaged was compelled to have his particular brand registered, and no brand was considered legal unless officially registered. Unbranded cattle were called mavericks, and as every man with a horse who was able to handle a rope and branding iron could brand them for his own profit, it was not long before every wild bovine had its legal owner.

It was on "maverick day" that we began our work for Collin Campbell, the cattle king.[1] One party had to build pens and enclosures near large grazing ranges, and the cattle were rounded up and kept ready for the drive to Kansas. I myself, with ten other cowboys—all of them Mexicans—was placed under the command of one John Doon. Our field of action was transferred to the country around the Escondido, Hondo, and Nueces creeks, west of the San Antonio River. With the exception of a few squatters who may have had reasons for hiding out because of facts best known to themselves, and some Mexican *jacales*, or huts made of adobe with thatched roofs, we rarely saw anybody, and the country was to all intents and purposes deserted. The appearance of this part of Texas was entirely different from any other part I had seen. Instead of trees there were only briars and yucca palms with flower stems six feet long and covered with large, waxy flower bells of an ivory whiteness. There were also gigantic cactus plants with their large, fleshy leaves, reaching a height of from ten to fifteen feet and growing in clusters so dense that they were almost impassable for horse and rider. Their leaves bristled with needles from one to two inches long, while their branches were resplendent with red or yellow or striped blossoms of the size and shape of an ordinary egg. Every available space left free by these plants was occupied by chaparral bushes, a description of which I have already given. Occasionally my horse would jump aside when it heard the threatening rattle of the rattlesnake. We could hear the enticing call of the partridge and gobble of the wild turkey, and on one occasion we sighted some antelope. Another time we saw three large herds of Texas deer crossing our way.

[1] V. F. Carvajal also recorded some of his adventures as a drover for Collin Campbell. See J. Marvin Hunter, *The Trail Drivers of Texas* (New York: Argosy-Antiquarian Ltd., 1963), II, 549–551, 839–842.

I never tired of admiring and enjoying the flowery wealth of the semitropical vegetation which seemed intended as a perpetual shelter to all the game thereabouts. But how different now is the sight of our former scene of action after the short space of fifty years!

It was not many years before an infectious disease called "black tongue" made away with many deer and antelope. The thousands of wild turkeys were exterminated by hunters who made it their business to kill them for profit. The soil is tilled now and nothing is to be seen but cotton and corn fields, which shows that a new civilization has taken possession of the country.

Toward evening we reached a creek which was our first camping place, and nearby was a spring of cool, clear water. This particular spot had years before served similar purposes and was arranged accordingly. There were pens and chutes for branding cattle. There were no houses, but after a ride of thirty-five miles we did not need any such accommodations. With only our saddles for pillows, and wrapped in our blankets with the starry sky of the South above us, we slept soundly and well.

We had taken a sufficient supply of provisions along to last us for supper and breakfast, and the following morning our provision wagon, commonly called the "chuck wagon," arrived. It had left the Campbell ranch a day and a half before in order to reach its destination over a better but considerably longer route. It was the regular two-horse wagon, the rear end provided with an upright box, provided with compartments. This box contained the necessary utensils—twelve tin plates, the same number of tin cups, knives and forks, a supply of coffee, common yellow sugar, a can of molasses, some powder and lead for bullets, salt, a dozen rough towels, and matches. A large sack of flour and several large sides of bacon were stowed away in the front part of the wagon, together with coarse woolen blankets and rain coats. Our Mexicans were more frugal, or rather their wants were fewer, as their many-colored serapes were all they needed. The driver of our chuck wagon was an old and reliable Negro, good and trustworthy like all the darkies who had been reared in slavery.

Our camp was pitched in the shade of a huge liveoak tree. Several of the boys were ordered to repair the corrals and pens, which had not been in use for many years. All these corrals were constructed on the same plan. A space large enough to hold about a thousand cattle was marked out and then the necessary number of mesquite posts were cut, all of equal length. The corrals had to be circular shaped to avoid the corners' being broken down during the stampedes. To cut one hundred posts was considered a good day's work for one man. When this was finished a trench three feet in depth was dug in the soft sandy soil, and the mesquite posts were set up. At a distance of five feet from the ground the posts were fastened together by long strips of green rawhide. For gate posts especially strong tree trunks were selected, and after the cattle were corralled the crossbars were secured by Manila ropes. Such ropes were also used to stake out our horses when grazing and were always within reach in sufficient quantities to meet any situation. In order to make it an easier task to corral the wild cattle which had never before seen a human being or entered a pen, another wing one hundred to two hundred feet long was erected at right angles with the gate.

Our cowboys finished all these repairs in one day and were given a day's rest for preparations. Many of our horses were yet to be shod, as the ground over which we had to travel was hard and stony.

My first day's work was devoted to our forty saddle horses. They had to be hobbled, and the wildest among them were fastened to the trees while grazing. The nutritious mesquite grass was all the food our horses received for their labors in our behalf. On the second day one of our Mexicans had to attend to the horses while the foreman or "boss" took me along to shoot a fat steer for our meat supply. After a short ride we spied an especially fine specimen weighing about twelve hundred pounds. Its long smooth horns fairly glistened in the sun. Under the protection of the bushes we were able to approach within two hundred paces when an exciting run began. We succeeded in separating or cutting the steer from the herd and chased it at full gallop in the direction of our camp. We unfastened our lassoes to rope the steer as near camp as possible, and as the boss had the strongest and best-trained horse and was only a hundred yards from the chuck wagon, the noose of his lasso alighted squarely on the horns of the running steer. His steed threw its full weight on its haunches, and with a single jerk the steer fell to the ground. John, our Negro cook, accustomed to similar incidents of ranch life and warned by the noise, hastened to our rescue with a loaded six-shooter and with a single shot killed the animal, thus ending this thrilling chase. Dismounting, we hastened to open the main artery of the steer's neck in order to bleed it profusely, and skinning and disemboweling it in quick succession, we soon suspended the four quarters from the limbs of a liveoak tree to cool during the night. The following morning, with the assistance of our cook, my portion of the work was preserving the meat. As fresh meat spoils quickly in the heat of this region, it is cut into slices a foot long and dried in the open air, and as the value of much of it was very small, only the best and most tender pieces were used. The pieces selected were thoroughly salted, sprinkled with pepper, and suspended from lassoes between the trees to dry. This was usually accomplished by the sun's rays in two or three days. Meat thus prepared has a delicious taste, and each cowboy always carried a piece of it in his saddlebags to partake of in an emergency. It also served as an improvised ration for supper when our camp could not be reached by meal time. But this kind of meat was never eaten in camp, as young cattle were slaughtered daily for a fresh supply; besides, our Negro cook killed deer and turkeys from time to time to provide us a greater variety of food.

Before a man becomes familiar with the wilderness he must become accustomed to many and various nocturnal noises. Twilight is very short in these latitudes and darkness sets in shortly after sunset. The beginning gloom generally discloses a truly wonderful sight: thousands of little fireflies come flitting through the air, especially on sultry nights, and other thousands of glowworms shed their tiny lights on the dark ground, affording an altogether glorious illumination of what I thought to be God's own country. Before we closed our eyes in slumber we could hear the various noises that mark the beginning of animal nightlife. The first creature to raise its voice was the whip-poor-will, ever repeating those three monotonous sounds from which it derives its name. Then our ears would be greeted by the melodious tunes of the mockingbird—the American nightingale—singing sweet and passionate strains and mocking the voices of the different creatures of the wilds. A little later the howling of the wolves would start, and they seemed always to be quite near when in fact they were miles away.

These wolves would never attack a human being, as calves and young cattle afforded an ever-ready repast for them. Many kinds of owls, big and little, attracted our attention by their calls and answers, for now was the time for them to begin their murderous attacks on the smaller birds sleeping peacefully upon their roosts. To this and much more the man of the wilderness becomes accustomed as easily as the city man becomes accustomed to the nocturnal noises of the city.

My pallet was near the one occupied by the foreman, and at night he would instruct me how to read the starry sky and how to determine the time by the position of the constellations. During the day the sun is the best index of the time. The sun remains visible about twelve hours. The hand of an adult with outstretched arm will cover one-twelfth of the normal course of the sun; thus it is easy to determine the hour of the day. At noon the sun is vertically above us; our shadow, therefore, is shortest. In bright moonlight the hours of the night are calculated in exactly the same way as during the day—namely—the width of the hand.

An hour before daybreak activity began in the camp. Our faithful Negro cook built a fire by sifting the live coals from the ashes and throwing the dry branches collected the evening before over them. Presently a bright flame would shoot up and the sleepers, having fully rested without undressing, pulling off only their boots, would arise hastily. From a tin cup one cowboy would pour water on the hands of another that he might wash his face and hands. The red handkerchief worn around the neck during the day would serve for a towel, and while the cook was preparing the coffee and frying the bacon, the cowboys would listen for the sound of the bells on their hobbled horses. It is truly remarkable how excellent and acute is the cowboy's sense of hearing, each one recognizing the sound of his particular bell regardless of the difference in tone. Before breakfast the horses are brought into camp and curried after a fashion by the use of corncobs. In a few minutes the mounts are saddled and ready to go. The breakfast is short and is consumed either while standing or squatting near the campfire. Each cowboy takes one large final drink of water, leaps into the saddle, and begins his hard twelve hours' work. The cook watched the remaining horses and he had plenty of time to do it as the boys seldom returned to camp before evening.

On this particular occasion it had been decided to round up from five to eight hundred cattle and deliver them at Ecleto Creek where Campbell had his headquarters. Shortly before sunrise and after a ride of six miles in a northerly direction, we espied five small herds of cattle which dispersed in all directions. Our work now started in real earnest. On our fast mounts we succeeded in getting some twenty mixed cattle and tried to keep them from the thick underbrush, but holding them was out of the question. They broke on all sides, but we finally surrounded them. It was now comparatively easy to keep the cows and heavier steers together, but when a young calf tried to escape we had to race our horses for hours in order to rope it. A regular cowboy knows better than anybody that a yearling calf can outrun almost any other animal on the globe. By noon we had caught about thirty head. The heat was excessive and, our work being very hard and trying, we were soon tormented by a burning thirst. As a canteen would have been very inconvenient on horseback, it was impossible to carry any drinking water during a round-up; we trusted, therefore, to our good luck in finding a creek to quench our thirst. Failing in this, we used to take the leaves of trees in our mouths to alleviate our suffering.

About two o'clock in the afternoon we reached a waterhole known well to our Mexicans, but it did not look inviting, because during the drought of that time a large number of horses and cattle had made frequent visits to the same place. We drank, nevertheless, and it tasted exceedingly fine to us as well as to our horses. For drinking vessels while on the road we used our great Mexican hats, called "sombreros." This kind of hat is very heavy, but it does not retard the growth of hair, as I do not ever recall seeing a bald-headed Mexican.

An hour later we experienced the first misfortune. An especially fine fat bull had repeatedly succeeded in slipping away from us and was trying to do so again when Pancho, one of our Mexicans, who was riding his fine Mexican pony, which he called Dulcis, in high spirits shouted: "Now watch how Dulcis is going to work." The bull was as fast as a horse and it required a long time for Pancho to get near enough to toss his lasso, which he did splendidly. His horse too performed well, but just the moment when Dulcis threw itself on its haunches the bull doubled a tree. Pancho, aware of the terrific danger, was trying to unfasten his lasso from the saddle horn when the bull reached the end of it, and the third and fourth fingers of his left hand were caught between saddle horn and lasso, the bones near the joint were broken, and flesh and skin crushed and lacerated. The bull fell on its knees and Pancho had presence of mind to jerk his ever-ready knife from its scabbard to cut the lasso. The bull, then free, jumped up and ran away with the lasso. Several days later we recaptured the bull but the fine lasso was gone. Pancho wrapped his hand in his handkerchief and followed our herd slowly to the camp. When we arrived there we experienced little difficulty in penning our little herd of about thirty head. We refreshed ourselves and rested besides the spring, meanwhile turning our attention to Pancho, who had just arrived. Our foreman removed the handkerchief from his hand and with a sharp pocket knife cut off the injured fingers at the joints. Needles and silk thread were to be found in every cow camp, so, covering the two stumps with the remaining skin, the foreman took a few stitches and, covering the wound with a salve made of tallow and kerosene, wrapped the hand in a clean bandage. In a few days Pancho was able to be on his horse and watch the herds again, but it was several months before he would attempt any lassoing.

These incidents, though trifling and possessing little human interest now, are related to show the hardships the cowboys of those days had to undergo.

It was now about four o'clock in the afternoon and we still had to brand the penned herd and ear-mark them. Immediately after our arrival we unsaddled our horses and turned them into the pasture. Dragging some large dry branches into the corral, we built a big fire and made the branding irons red hot. The brand of the owner could be applied to the shoulders, ribs, or hips of the animal, but when a herd was to be moved out of the state a special brand had to be used and imprinted on the hips near the backbone. We did our work hurriedly. The yearlings were crowded into small herds, and one of the boys would rush upon the nearest animal and, pushing his right hand into its mouth, would grasp the lower jaw and with his left hand seize a horn, and after he jerked the beast's neck to the left, another cowboy would get a tail-hold and down the animal came. A third cowboy was ready with the red-hot iron which was then deeply burnt into the skin, but care had to be taken not to burn the flesh too deep, as wounds of this kind are difficult to heal. Big steers and strong bulls had to be treated differently, as they would sometimes attack their captors. But similar methods were used in getting large animals on the ground and the rest was easy.

Our work was over before sundown. We left the animals penned up during the night, carefully fastening and securing all gates. We then had a general cleanup at the spring and were ready for our frugal supper with real appetites, as we had worked all day without dinner. When not too tired we would all gather around the bright campfire which the cook always kept supplied with fuel, and in turn each member of our outfit would give an account of his exploits and experiences. Sometimes humor had its fling and funny stories were told, but they were always kept within the bounds of decency. John, the Negro cook, was the happy owner of an old guitar which he carried along on the chuck wagon, and being musical like all Negroes he entertained us by singing those old Negro songs, some sad, others gay, and accompanying well on the instrument. By the aid of his instructions I soon acquired a certain skill in handling the guitar, but I preferred to accompany the Mexican singers with their sweet melodies, and after much practice I learned to play the fandango, the Mexican national dance. This brought new life to our camp, as most of our dusky rough-riders were excellent and graceful dancers and enjoyed this form of recreation henceforth every evening.

On one occasion some rough-looking individuals passed the night in our camp. I later learned that they were fugitives from the law and were hiding out on account of various murders they had committed. They told us they had discovered traces of the Comanche Indians, so thereafter one-half of our outfit had to watch our horses nightly. Fortunately our apprehensions were not realized, and after several days of suspense we returned to our daily routine.

A few days later two of our Mexicans who had been sent out on a scouting tour to a neighboring settlement near the Nueces

River returned with the news that they had found freshly made mustang pony tracks a few miles from the camp. Catching mustangs was a sport every man was fond of in those days, so two of our Mexican cowboys were given a leave of absence for a two days' hunt, and I was permitted by the boss to join the party. Besides provisions we were provided with a dozen loops made of rope, but how these loops were to be used I had not the faintest idea. After we had selected the best saddle horses, we started in search of the mustang tracks, and about five miles from the camp in a plain bordered by a thick underbrush we heard some of these ponies whinnying for their colts. Upon this discovery our horses grew nervous and it was only with difficulty that they could be restrained, so we let them have the rein, but in a moment the mustangs had trooped together. Two young stallions led the advance guard of the herd, which amounted to about thirty head. The oldest and in all probability the strongest of the herd of mustangs brought up the rear ranks.

Those who have never had the good fortune to see a herd of mustangs have no idea of the beautiful sight these creatures afford when, with flying manes and trailing tails, they sweep like a hurricane across the plains. We followed them in a wild chase for probably eight miles before we drew our reins to rest our horses. The mustangs too lessened their speed, but their endurance and strength remained unimpaired. The stallions furiously pawed the ground and their neighing sounded like the blasts of trumpets. We followed them as they sped on, racing and resting our horses in turn, until in the afternoon my companions decided on a new line of attack. In a thickly wooded valley they had discovered a clearing dotted here and there with trees. After an extensive circuit, lest we be scented by the mustangs, we reached the desired spot. Our twelve rope loops were arranged about six feet from the ground and fastened to some of the strongest branches of the trees. This stratagem was based on the fact that horses shrink from running through dense thickets. Our trap arranged, we stole back to our former position, returning by the same circuitous route, and renewed the chase. We succeeded in running our game right into the trap, and three of them were caught in the treacherous loops. The first mustang broke his neck by the terrific shock; the second escaped by breaking the rope; but the third stallion remained safe and intact, struggling wildly in the encircling loop and biting and pitching incessantly. We wished to take him to our camp, but after one of my Mexican companions climbed the tree to slacken the loop so as not to strangle the mustang, the latter suddenly reared on its hind legs and grasped the cowpuncher's arm with his teeth, whereupon the other Mexican, realizing the situation in a flash, brought the mustang stallion down with a well-aimed shot.

This concluded the first and last mustang hunt of which I was ever a witness or in which I participated. Our horses were very tired, so we camped near a waterhole close by and on the next afternoon returned to camp without our coveted trophy.

Often I have been asked by later settlers what became of those immense herds of mustangs, and I wish to state right here that most of them were shot and killed, as they could not be utilized for practical purposes. Rarely if ever has one of these animals been so tamed that it remained permanently gentle. Even when broken and mounted by expert horsemen, they soon returned to their wild pranks, bucking and running away when they were most urgently needed. When the settlers of these wilds later began to breed better stock, they frequently encountered these mustangs, which invariably caused damage to themselves and their horses.

It was not only the Mexicans who greatly spoiled me by their affectionate friendship, but my boss was also fond of giving me many hours of pleasure and leisure. Many an afternoon I was allowed to go hunting or to practice target shooting with pistol and rifle to improve my marksmanship, and in time I was able to perform all the duties of a regular cowboy. I could ride and manage almost any horse, and day by day new events transpired which sustained my interest.

What first claimed my attention and wonder was the great number and variety of poisonous animals. Frequently I encountered the prairie snake and watched it glide through the grass as swiftly as a good horse can trot. The entire region I found abounding in rattlesnakes. The specimens killed by us were from three to seven years old, a fact which could be learned from the rattles, every link of which represents one year. We had but two extraordinarily large rattlers in our collection, the smaller one containing twelve rattles, the larger one sixteen. Rattlesnakes are lazy and move about slowly. When one approaches them, they coil up into a ring and, raising their heads about a foot, give the danger signal by shaking their rattles. A very remarkable snake found in western Texas is the king snake. It is only a foot and a half long and about the size of a man's thumb, but it is not poisonous. It seems, however, to have been created for the extermination of the large venomous reptiles and to be immune from all the various poisons. Its skin too is of remarkable beauty, being marked with alternate rings of a bright red, yellow, and black. Upon scenting a venomous serpent, this little creature steals up to it noiselessly and, rushing with unerring aim, encircles the throat of its adversary, gradually contracting its coils until the victim is strangled. Other loathsome creatures which make the country unsafe are the hairy tarantula, a venomous spider, and the centipede, an articulated animal about eight inches in length with numerous feet equipped with poison fangs. It is a fact little short of a miracle that, considering the great number of these venomous pests, comparatively few persons are injured and killed by snakes and other noxious vermin.

In a few weeks we had rounded up six hundred beeves, and as they were watched all day, they soon became accustomed to human company. Many a wild steer, however, had escaped us and fled into the dense cactus thickets. They were large, valuable animals and hard to recover, as it was next to impossible to rope them among these thickets. But we employed the following strategy, which actually enabled us to add fifty more of these bovines to our herd. During the day the steers would hide in the thickets, but at night they came out for grazing. It was our favorite sport to rope them by moonlight and leave them hobbled, and the next morning we would drive our herd past their resting place and they were glad to join the herd after we had removed the thongs from their tired and stiff limbs. In the meantime our cook had brought some tame oxen from a ranch ten miles distant. To these the meanest steers were linked and made secure. The last days we spent in cutting out a small herd of the gentlest steers, and every morning we had them pass through these thickets where we hoped to find more steers. We would then frighten these wild creatures with whoops, shots, and other violent noises, which, by the way, was dangerous for ourselves and our horses, so that those which could not be caught by the lasso generally remained and joined the other beasts.

The cactus thickets so often mentioned contained a great many dead trees, decayed and fallen because the rapidly growing brambles robbed them of their proper nourishment. During our mad chases over their branches many a mount with its rider tumbled down, but fortunately we never sustained any serious injuries. Most disagreeable of all were the hundreds of cactus needles which pierced our skin and had to be removed at night by the aid of our campfire, one comrade doing this charitable service for another.

After a month of untold hardships we had rounded up a herd of more than 750 head, but some of them bearing brands of ranchers living near had to be cut out. In this task our intelligent horses did the most important part. The herd was crowded together in an open space and kept there by mounted cowboys riding circle. Two men now invaded the herd and indicated to their horses the steers to be removed, by urging them as near as possible to the desired animals. Soon the intelligent horse knows what it is to do. It keeps close to the marked steer even in the densest crowd, biting it on its back to make it move faster and leaping from one side to the other until it has crowded the steer out of the herd. It is a difficult task for the horse because the steer is unwilling to break loose from the herd and tries to return by all manner of tricks. Naturally the entire herd becomes excited and mills around, but the boys at the outskirts prevent any stampede. Admirable also is the indescribable skill of the horse in shielding the rider from injury, even going so far as to avoid a low branch likely to unhorse him, or sometimes leaping a ditch or jumping over a rock or intervening bushes, but never losing sight of the fleeing steer which the cowboy is hotly pursuing.

Before I tell the reader how we left the country on the trail back to the Campbell ranch, I should like to call attention to a remarkable animal now also rendered extinct by the progress of civilization. It is the muskhog or peccary, also called "javelina." This species of wild hog usually attains a weight of about sixty-five pounds; they flock together in droves and their skin is provided with hard bristles not unlike needles. On the back near the tail is the musk-secreting gland that gives the animal its name. Its tusks are extraordinarily long and its flesh is not fit for human consumption, as it has the strong taste and odor of its musky secretion. Living as they do in droves of forty to fifty, these animals are among the most courageous in existence. At the approach of a drove of these wild hogs or javelinas, cattle and horses will flee in all directions. Our Negro cook, who was ignorant of the ferocity of the wild hogs, shot one when he was rabbit hunting. The entire pack turned on him and he was forced to climb a tree and remain there until sundown.

Innumerable encounters with these strange beasts were related around our campfire, and the numerous javelina skins about us left no doubt as to the authenticity of some of these tales.

I had received permission to spend the last four days during which our herd was pastured on a hunting expedition, and one of our Mexicans, himself an old hunter, was permitted to act as my companion. My *compadre* had been reared in the wilderness, and he taught me how to find and follow the tracks of the manifold game. We had been so busy with our daily routine that I had no conception of the abundance of wild animals thriving in the depths of the thickets. The small prairie wolves (coyotes) were not dangerous at all, although they roamed in packs. It was different, though, with the great gray wolves called "lobos," which were fond of horseflesh and seized and killed many a young colt. They generally hunted in pairs and when hungry did not shrink from attacking even larger beeves and other animals. But the strongest and largest beast of prey, excepting the black bear, is beyond doubt the Texas jaguar; unfortunately we never met one, although we saw their tracks. Their average weight was estimated to be several hundred pounds. One night my companion roused me that I might listen to the cry of the mountain lion, or puma, which is said to be a cowardly animal but becomes dangerous when wounded. With the wildcats, or catamounts, which were very numerous, we had better luck. We succeeded in killing two specimens, a male and female, and brought their skins to the camp. It struck me while looking at their skins that their stripes were very different in arrangement because, unlike the tiger's, their stripes ran lengthwise, not crosswise. The male specimen weighed about fifty pounds, its mate about thirty-five.

Excellent objects for target practice were the numerous chaparral cocks, which were about the size of pheasants. We could easily shoot them with our rifles, as they seldom used their wings for flight although they can outrun a horse. The deer, however, with its graceful motions and white, bushy tail was doubtless the most beautiful creature we encountered. We did not like to kill them except when in need of venison; but many a time we chased them on horseback and easily caught up with them when the country was reasonably open. The smaller animals such as opossums, polecats (skunks), civet cats, squirrels, and jackrabbits we left in peace, for the reason that our munitions were too precious to be wasted on them.

Cattle Drive

WE started finally on our trip to join the herd at the ranch headquarters. Our horses were terribly tired and, all our precautions to the contrary, some of them had galls and could not be used for some time. Others had become lame by leaping over tree stumps and ditches or by cactus needles piercing their knees and fetlock joints. Nevertheless, everything went well. We had selected an open route which led us past ranches where we could use the corrals to keep our herds together during the night. But one night something frightened our herd and, wild with terror, our cattle rushed against the corral's enclosure. A section of the heavy posts was broken down in a moment, but we rushed to the scene and succeeded in repulsing the terror-stricken animals. On the fourth day we reached Campbell's ranch and merged our herd with those already corralled at the ranch headquarters. We received our wages and a few days furlough to rest and recover before we started on the move to Kansas.

We now paid a parting visit to Helena to get rid of our hard-earned money as fast as possible. The most alluring objects of our wishes were fancy boots with many-colored legs and elegant fringes on top. Next, red silk sashes were purchased to adorn our waists. Munitions too were bought and whatever else was necessary or attracted our fancies. Copious drafts of whiskey were taken, which led to a cutting affray between our Mexicans while I was attending an American dance. For this occasion a good-sized room in the hotel in Helena was selected. The music was furnished by a violin, but when it could not be heard on account of the noise, the dancers kept time with their feet. Round dances like the waltz and polka were unknown in this part of the country, so the people enjoyed square dances, especially the Virginia reel. A so-called prompter called out the different figures and the dancers executed them with consummate skill. In another room card playing went on for high stakes, and as whiskey was consumed in generous proportions, the dance ended as usual—a young rancher being shot down by a rival in a fit of jealousy. Even when dancing these people never parted with their six-shooters and Bowie knives.

We now made our preparations for the move north, estimated to last four months—three months for the northward drive and one month for the return trip—the entire distance to the point of delivery being more than a thousand miles. One of my favorite saddle horses was unfit for work and had to be replaced by another mount.

This was the time when Texas was beginning to be slowly settled. The chief occupation was still the cattle business. Even during dry years when grass was scarce cattle could be fed on cactus leaves, which grew everywhere, and despite the fact that numerous needles kept sticking in the mouths and tongues of the animals, the cattle were fond of returning to the cactus patches. In later years and especially when there was a grass famine, the needles were singed off and the cattle remained sound and well fed. Still later people were sent out with gasoline torches to singe the needles without the necessity of cutting and carrying the leaves to the fire. With the growing population, the demand for Texas cattle steadily increased in Kansas, and as our cattle could withstand great heat and the rigors of the northern winters, provided they were kept in good condition in autumn, great cattle ranches were established in the north and stocked with Texas cattle.

The pioneers who moved the first great herds to the north did so under many disadvantages and only after many hardships. There were no established routes, and to obtain the necessary quantity of water, they had to go great distances out of the way. The cattlemen who had already settled in northern Texas forbade them to pass through their territory, as the thousands of cattle quickly made away with their grass and trampled the roots into the ground, so that a new growth required a long time. In addition to these difficulties it frequently happened that the cowboys were killed or wounded by the arrows of some marauding Lipan or Comanche Indian. In those days the Indians had no other weapons but bows and arrows, and the few who possessed firearms either did not know how to use them to advantage or were unable to get ammunition for them. During rainy weather the bows were of no avail; indeed, the material used for bowstrings relaxed on account of the moisture. But under favorable conditions there are no more formidable weapons, and I have frequently seen some friendly Lipan shoot a coin from between the fingers of a tribesman at a distance of several paces. I have often witnessed flint-head arrows pierce a buffalo entirely, provided it was not diverted by coming in contact with a bone.

After a regular and permanent market for Texas cattle had been established in Kansas, the beeves were driven over better and more direct routes or trails. A Scotchman by the name of John Chisholm laid out the most direct route from Wichita on the Kansas frontier to the marketplaces of that state. Before that time the old buffalo trails had been used, but now the cattlemen began to use more direct routes south of Wichita, and present-day cattlemen know the route thus established and have passed thousands of cattle over the Old Chisholm Trail.

Several days would frequently elapse in cutting out the weaker animals which were not considered strong enough to stand the long and tiresome journey northward. Two more days were lost when brand inspectors appointed by the government made a list of all the brands to determine what foreign brands were in our herd, thereby enabling the owners to reclaim their equivalent after the sale of the cattle and the return of the cattlemen. For our herd sixteen cowboys had been engaged, one man for every hundred cattle, but three of these boys had to accompany the drove for only a hundred miles just to give the herd a good start, then they were free to return. I was one of the three, and we took only two saddle horses with us, as these were able to stand the hardships for a single week. To the other boys sixty good mounts were assigned, a great many more than were actually needed, but it was natural to expect that some would become disabled on the trail and that others would be stolen by the Indians. For our provisions an especially strong chuck wagon was selected and four mules hitched to it, for, as a matter of fact, aside from a considerable quantity of provisions and supplies, drinking water had to be included, as we had to pass through deserts where for maybe a day not a single drop of water was to be found. Of course our cattle and horses suffered terribly from thirst during such long drives and some actually died. I have often noticed that on occasions such as this the poor suffering animals were able to scent the water at a distance of six to eight miles, and they no sooner scented it than the entire herd plunged headlong and could not be stopped until it had reached the water and quenched its thirst.

We started our journey without any trouble. Our herd was headed by our boss. Four or five men rode along the sides, and as many cowboys brought up the rear. It was not very long before the strongest animals were in front and had to be restrained, while the weaker ones lagged behind.

Our road was hedged in by large bushy tracts; therefore, it was the safest way for fifteen hundred head distributed over a space of a half a mile. No cowboy enjoys accompanying such a drove because it does not afford any change or variety whatever, and it is otherwise disagreeable on account of the dust raised by the thousands of hooves. It enters the lungs and parches the mouth and tongue in spite of the fact that the mouth and nose are covered with handkerchiefs.

So the long trail wends its way until perhaps by noon a brook appears, watering the grazing grounds where the hungry and fagged animals can find rest and food for a few hours. The journey is then continued until evening, when preparations for the night rest of the herd must be made. This is accomplished in this manner: after having reached a level and open part of the country, the herd is surrounded by all the cowboys and crowded into the smallest possible space. For many hours the boys continue to circle around the herd, keeping the same distance apart but contracting the circles more and more. At the same time they have to shout certain long-drawn monotonous tunes called "songs" intended to lull the cattle to sleep. When a majority of the cattle have lain down, half of the crew can go to the chuck wagon for supper while the other half must ride circle until midnight.

The first party at the camp saddle fresh horses, lie down on the ground without undressing, and snatch a few hours of sleep, after which they relieve their partners who have held the herd until midnight. The latter now partake of supper at the chuck wagon and, after saddling fresh mounts, go to rest. The saddled horses must be kept near so that the cowboy can leap into the saddle at the least suspicious motion of the herd and come to the assistance of his comrades on duty. This kind of life is endurable so long as every- thing goes as smoothly as I have described it here, and a sleep of four or five hours is sufficient to restore the strength of a sound man, according to my experience. But at times it rains at night, the cow- boys get soaking wet, and to get a few hours of night rest they have to lie down on the wet ground wrapped in wet blankets. In bad weather the work and hardships are redoubled; the herd grows restless, and it cannot be seen during dark and rainy nights; no- body gets a chance to rest, and the poor horses are nearly killed by overwork. Nor is this the worst part. At night the cattle are nervous and timid and likely to be struck with blind terror by the least noise which they are not accustomed to hear. The entire herd plunges into the darkness as if chased by the furies, in pouring rain or beat- ing hail, while the cowboy, bound to remain with his herd, tries to get ahead of it, racing over bushes and rocks in a country unknown to him, leaping creeks, dodging low branches, and seeing only a part of his herd during blinding lightning flashes, while he has to depend on his ears to detect the direction taken by the majority of the stampeding cattle. In such moments a horseman learns to love his horse because it is his horse which saves him from destruction, seeing at night as well as in the daytime. It leaps over every hole and rock the cowboy cannot see and instinctively avoids trees, the low branches of which threaten to pierce him any instant; it speeds over the soft ground ahead of the herd without ever losing its foot- ing, thereby saving the rider's life again, because in case of a fall horse and rider would be trampled to death by the senseless stam- peding cattle in the rear. All this and more the horse performs with a sure instinct and almost superhuman intelligence, provided the horseman keeps it from stumbling by holding the reins tight.

For hours the cattle run about trembling with fear, and when they begin to settle down to a short rest, any strange noise may stampede them again and again until the day dawns. At daybreak the herd is sometimes found eight or ten miles from camp; none of the boys knows the whereabouts of the chuck wagon; no house or settlement is to be seen for miles around; and the poor and hard-used horse has to carry its master for another day without rest, saddled and unfed. The cowboy too is longing for a bite of food and a drink of hot coffee. But he must wait, sometimes till night, until the chuck wagon has been found. After the first stampede the cattle continue to be nervous for days, and nightly stampedes may continue indefinitely. I have seen able-bodied men fall from their horses in the deep sleep of exhaustion after such experiences and continue to sleep on the ground without even being awakened by the fall.

It may not be uninteresting for the reader to find here the description of another frequent cause of stampedes in winter—our so-called Texas northers—icy storms from the north which generally set in after oppressive heat and cause the mercury to fall from summer heat to freezing point in a few short hours. It must be remembered that such a rapid change of temperature would burst the strongest steam boiler, yet our cattle had to stand it without any other protection than the winter coat given them by nature.

The Texas norther reaches its height when it changes into a sleet norther, that is, when it is accompanied by a drizzling rain that turns into ice while descending. In a short time the earth is covered with a sheet of ice; rivers and water pools freeze; the birds freeze on their roosts in the trees. In the cities and towns water-pipes burst and the flowers droop and perish; all outside work ceases, and man entrenches himself behind a hot stove while all other unprotected animals undergo great suffering. On the open prairie where they cannot find refuge in the cover of trees or under-brush, the cattle begin to drift, and with heads hanging low to protect them from the icy blasts they slowly succumb to the storm, and singly or in droves head southward until they find shelter or until a river or, in later years, a wire fence, stops their advance. Then they crowd together, an impenetrable mass, rendered helpless by the icy cold of the polar current. The weaker animals and those most exposed to the elements and sometimes even the whole herd freeze to death, and the cowboy riding in search of his cattle after the norther has abated may congratulate himself if he finds his herd intact, although miles away from their original grazing ground.

After such a norther as described, Texas steers several years old that were owned in Palo Pinto County have been found on the headwaters of the Nueces River in Uvalde County, three hundred miles from home. Amidst storms like these the animals are naturally restless and easily frightened, and the fall of a rock, the sudden flight of a bird, or the movement of a rabbit may cause the most disastrous stampede.

The reader may ask how it is possible for these icy winds to strike a subtropical country with such fury. In answer I may state that this abnormal condition is caused by the singular arrangement of the American mountain ranges—the Sierra Nevada, the Cascade and Rocky Mountains in the West, and the Appalachian Mountains in the East, all sweep in a north-south direction, thus leaving between them the Great Central Plain and affording for the cold air current a huge corridor to the North Pole from the Gulf of Mexico. This situation has been aggravated by the indiscriminate devastation of the forests which once covered a great part of the United States and Canada, and formed a natural barrier against those north storms.

As it had been decided not to use the Chisholm Trail but another more easterly route, we were headed for Austin, which, although the capitol of the state, was not a large city at that time. Before we reached the place we had to swim our great herd across the Guadalupe River, which had risen very high. To avoid the raging current, in which many of the smaller animals might have perished, we selected a place where the river was very wide and consequently the water less swift. It was about five miles north of the little town of Gonzales. In two hours time our entire herd had safely crossed the river. We cowboys now passed over on horseback, but our chuck wagon had to make a detour of ten miles to find a safe ford for crossing. *All told we were fifteen men besides old Jim Hackney, who drove the camp wagon and attended to the cooking. I think we had a herd of fifty saddle horses, so when all hands were mounted, thirty-five loose horses had to be herded, to which we attended alternately. When my day came, we had just received a few wild, unbroken horses to take the place of a few who were down and out. In roping up these new ones, I slipped on the wet ground, got entangled in the loops of the rope, and the strong horse dragged me about two hundred yards through the Guadalupe* bottom and the rope cut deep into my leg. *We bandaged the wounds with old towels soaked in axle grease, but they continued to remain very painful.* Five days later we reached the Colorado River near Austin. It is indeed considerably longer and wider than the Guadalupe, but since it had not rained as much here, we could easily cross it about two miles above the city. When we reviewed and recounted our herd we were glad to find that we had lost only eighteen head, which was lucky for us, all things considered.

Above Austin the country became very brushy, and as I ran cattle back into the herd, my sores were always torn open again, and I thought it best to leave the herd and the job. I did not want to return to Emily with empty hands, and learning that I was only about one hundred miles from San Saba, the land of my dreams, I went there in the hope of better employment and of meeting the wild Indians face to face.

The Colorado Country

I had now fulfilled the duties agreed upon in my contract, and after I had received my salary I was free to visit San Saba, a place I had long wished to see, as it is one of the most interesting spots in the state. This little city is situated on the banks of the San Saba River, from which both town and county take their names. The time I spent in the place, not quite two years, I consider to be the most interesting of all my life—or it may be just because it was full of dangers, but at the same time varied and romantic.

Human habitations were scarce and only to be found along the rivers, but the people inhabiting them were real men, shirking no work and absolutely without fear. The savage Comanche Indians still considered themselves the rulers of this country, but these hardy pioneers made short work in repelling them and conquering the region for themselves.

Leaving Austin, I followed the path along the Colorado River and often was near enough to see its red waters. This red color which gave the river its name (Rio Colorado—Red River) is caused by deposits of dark red clay through which the river has to traverse for a long way. Continuing my journey, I passed from the level prairie into the hill country, great stretches of which were covered with a growth of mountain cedar. These cedar forests, being almost impassable, were a safe retreat for many beasts of prey. Advancing farther, I met with high limestone rocks, until suddenly I discovered myself in the granite formations of Burnet County. This primeval formation, about forty miles square, had been raised to the surface at some antediluvian period through different strata of limestone.

The mountains of this county are therefore of fantastic shapes and wonderful beauty. The iron which exists in large quantities in the sand causes all vegetation to be of a dark green color in this granite formation, giving the country a somber and melancholy aspect. The sands of its creeks are to some extent auriferous, but very often it is the tinsel only that glitters in the sun. One of the mountains, nearly a mile in diameter, seems almost of solid iron. Parts of it can be worked and hammered on the anvil. A chemical analysis of one mass proved it to be 68.72 percent pure iron, but unfortunately there is no coal within several hundred miles, neither were there at that time any railroads, which are indispensable for the development of any industry. However, these mountains of pure granite are now being utilized and furnish slabs of a fine red color which are susceptible to a high polish.

Riding through the streets of Austin, the capitol city of Texas, on my way to San Saba, I was astonished to find it so primitive in appearance. There was one main street, lined with many one-story buildings that did not appear very city-like. The state capitol, which should be the pride and ornament of every American capital city, looked like an ordinary residence and burned down one year later.[1] The members of the legislature, foreseeing the bright future of their country, were then willing to have a capitol building worthy of the great state of Texas, but the necessary funds were lacking. A great Chicago wholesale firm finally proposed to build the present edifice for three million acres of land and sent a Mr. Wilke, a German architect, to Austin to execute the work.[2] He was a long time in finding suitable material for the construction of the capitol, until he decided to build a narrow-gauge railroad to the Granite Mountain and utilize Texas granite. The iron framework for the gigantic cupola was ordered from Belgium, as the freight rates from the American iron works were prohibitive. And at this juncture another obstacle materialized: there were no stonecutters available to work the hard granite, so a hundred Scotch workmen had to be imported, as there were none to be had in America. Sometime previous the

[1] The capitol burned November 9, 1881.
[2] Gus Wilke was a subcontractor for the capitol; E. E. Myers of Detroit was the architect. See *The Texas Capitol: Symbol of Accomplishment* (Austin: Texas Legislative Council and Texas Highway Department, 1967), pp. 31, 39.

labor unions in the states had put through an immigration law placing a fine of one thousand dollars on every imported contract-worker. Mr. Wilke was therefore fined one hundred thousand dollars for his one hundred stonecutters and had to pay, in addition to the fine, their passage across the ocean and return.

The present Texas capitol is one of the most beautiful and substantial edifices in the United States, and one which every Texan may be proud of.

I now left the granite country behind and continued my way in the direction of San Saba. To the northwest of Lampasas I found small prairies alternating with large cedar forests, and toward evening of the first day I came to a community consisting of a few log houses called Wolf's Settlement. It was a small cattle ranch owned by a Mr. Wolf and his sons.[3] When I asked for directions concerning my way, the old gentleman invited me to pass the night with them, as the Comanche Indians were on the warpath against the people of San Saba and it was not safe to camp out in the open.

Wolf's sons had been sent out to bring in the few saddle horses they possessed. It was the custom of the ranchers to tie their horses to an open log cabin during the night for protection. Accepting the invitation to spend the night, I dismounted and left my horses grazing near the house, intending to tie them to the log cabin at sundown. But when I went to fetch them an hour later I could not find them anywhere; however, toward ten o'clock that night the best one of my horses voluntarily returned and was tied to Mr. Wolf's house. An hour later we were roused by the loud call of neighbors living five miles north of the settlement, and they told us that all their horses had been stolen by the Comanches that evening. We tried to enlist the aid of as many people as possible in the recovery of their stock from the redskins.

We decided to take up their trail at dawn and to notify all squatters who could be reached to come to Wolf's Settlement be-

[3] Probably George W. Wolf, a pioneer Methodist preacher, farmer, and rancher of Llano County. His daughter, Mrs. Sarah Rebecca Jane Wolf Pearl, recorded some of her reminiscences of the era in N. H. Pierce, comp., *The Free State of Menard: A History of the County* (Menard, Texas: Western Advertising Company, 1975), pp. 168–169.

fore daybreak. Mr. Wolf, the father, was an old hunter and experienced Indian fighter, so he was put in command of the expedition. We took turns in watching our horses with especial care while Mother Wolf prepared coffee for us. Before morning four more men arrived who wished to join Father Wolf, one of his sons, and myself in the pursuit. The other son remained to protect his mother.

After a search of about two hours we discovered the fresh tracks of possibly twenty horses, nearly all of them shod. As the Indians never had their horses shod, we were sure they were the tracks of our own stolen animals. We could see plainly that about fifteen horses had been running in a straight line, while five of them had left their tracks in a kind of zigzag arrangement. We inferred that these belonged to the Indians who were hurrying on the herd. We now put our horses into a gallop, and a little later when we had reached a large waterhole we knew we were going in the right direction, for we discovered footprints of Indian moccasins where the horse thieves had quenched their thirst. We dismounted for a few minutes, tightened cinches, and after a careful examination of our arms took up the trail again.

Father Wolf, our leader, told us that the Indians, being fewer in number, were trying to reach the nearest cedar forest three miles away where they would have a reasonable chance of defending themselves. So it was imperative that we reach the Indians while they were in the open and make good use of our firearms. We knew the Indians had nothing but bows and arrows, so we put spurs to our horses. But before we could overtake the Comanches, two of them had already reached the cedar forest with our horses, and the remaining three had found a safe hiding place behind trees and were ready to put up a fight. Their position was about a hundred yards ahead of us and was more advantageous than ours. Some arrows came whizzing past us and we fired several shots, without, however, doing any more damage than knocking the bark off the trees. We had left our horses with one of our men who had removed them a hundred yards from the scene of action. They were restless and were of no use to us at this stage of the fight. Beyond our enemies we saw an Indian mounted on horseback holding three more horses by their reins. As the arrows came in our direction less frequently, we now assumed their supply was limited and had to be disposed of sparingly. Suddenly we noticed one of the redskins sinking to the ground. Immediately the two who remained unhurt hastened to the aid of their comrade and, dragging him along in all haste, mounted their horses and disappeared.

We held a brief consultation and were considering whether it would be advisable to follow the Indians into the cedar brakes, because it was evident that these five were members of an organized band temporarily detached from a larger body of redskins and sure to rejoin it, when suddenly a troop of our stolen horses came running toward us. We hastily remounted in order to catch them, and we were glad to find upon close examination that we had recovered seventeen out of a total of twenty head, in addition to two Indian ponies. After a second consultation we decided to accept the loss of a single horse, which was practically worthless, rather than incur further hazards. I was surprised to find among the horses recovered my own favorite mount and the same one which I had been unable to find the evening before, but which I had not even thought of during the excitement of that hunt.

The horses were now distributed among the members of the expedition, and as we parted every man made the shortest cut to reach his home. The members of the hospitable Wolf family insisted that I remain with them for some days, or at least until the moon waned, as it was only on moonlight nights that the Indians made their raids in this part of the country, and as they were instantly pursued by the settlers, they seldom tarried longer than a few days.

Father Wolf had passed ten years of his life in these solitary wilds, and many were the skirmishes he had had with the redskins. His eldest son had been killed and scalped by the Comanches, and in the course of their regular raids they had stolen enough horses from him to keep him poor.[4]

During my short stay with the family I was regaled with so many bloodthirsty stories that, on continuing my journey to San Saba, I expected to find a skulking Indian behind every rock and bush and even dreamed of them at night.

---

[4] Mrs. Pearl recalled that her brother Wash Wolf was killed by Indians and her brother Hiram was taken captive but escaped (ibid., p. 168).

I proceeded along the Colorado River to the point where it merges with the clear waters of San Saba Creek. For miles the waters of these two streams run side by side until they meet at last in a single stream.

San Saba

WHEN I first arrived at San Saba I thought it to be a regular fairy-land. The river, clear as crystal, leaped and rippled for long stretches over white stone rocks through which it had eroded its way in the course of centuries. Again it passed peacefully between high banks and through rich black soil. The adjoining valleys were covered for miles with pecan trees bringing forth such an abundance of the finest nuts that they were not fully appreciated but were used as food for the half-wild hogs. In no part of the country did I see as many clear, cool springs as in this section. Some of them descending from the hills nearby passed on their way to the river over rich cultivated soil and were used by the settlers to irrigate their lands.

The inhabitants of this district differed as much in character from those people I had met in the past as their country differed from the places I had seen so far. The majority—not more than a hundred families—were immigrants from Kentucky and Tennessee, some of them farmers, some hunters, some cattle raisers, but all of them people of unflinching courage, because it was no child's play to settle with their families in this wilderness. Every one of them went about heavily armed. The two six-shooters in their belts were never missing, but in the place of the Spencer carbine or Enfield gun, they handled those long and heavy Kentucky and Tennessee rifles. These weapons were never used, however, for wanton murder at frivolous drinking bouts but served only to protect the pioneers in their endless encounters with the most atrocious Indian tribe that ever infested any country.

The tragedy I witnessed during the very first hours of my visit to San Saba induced me to remain there for several years and make myself as useful as I possibly could. After breakfast I left Mr. Mc-Anell's hospitable home near the junction of the San Saba and Colorado rivers. About three hours later I saw a small log cabin near the river and standing in front of it a half-dozen men. I approached the house partly because I was curious to find out what had happened and partly to ask directions about my road, but as everybody appeared to be too excited to pay any attention to me, I entered the cabin together with the other people. A terrible spectacle met our eyes. We found a small family weltering in blood, the father having been shot and scalped, the head of a boy about four years of age almost severed from the body, and the mother and daughter mutilated in an indescribable manner, while an older daughter had been kidnapped by the Indians. This brutal murder has been committed a few hours before, and all the men in the neighborhood for miles around had been called to arms by mounted messengers to begin the pursuit of the murderers, some of them arriving at that very moment.

While waiting, I helped to nail together some simple coffins, and as there was no more I could do, I continued on my way to San Saba. In the evening we received word that the murderous gang had been overtaken and that part of them had paid with their lives for the atrocities they had committed. The captured girl had been rescued and returned unhurt.

Hitherto I had traveled all alone, but now I decided to join with others on the road, as the Indians had not retreated any farther than the Concho River and there was constant danger of their coming upon us unawares.

Henderson's Ranch had been described to me as one of the finest places in the country, and when a few days later William Taylor, an old hunter and trapper, left with his eighteen-year-old son for the place where they owned a little cabin, I joined them. Young Taylor, who was almost my own age, became my best and almost inseparable companion.

The old hunter was a taciturn man, but Bill, the son, was fond of telling me of his hunting exploits, and I gladly accepted his invitation to join him and Ike Black,[1] his brother-in-law, in a buffalo hunt that was to take place the following week.

Present-day people have no conception how primitive was the life of these early settlers. The little cabin made of logs piled one upon the other contained but a single room. It had no door, only an opening in its place, no window or wood floor. It served as a dwelling place for husband, wife, and four daughters. The old couple slept in a rudely constructed bed. Its frame was covered with straps of rawhide, and on it lay an under-bed stuffed with corn-shucks and covered with a woolen blanket. The girls slept on the ground on similar under-beds, so at night the entire floor (consisting of the bare ground) was occupied. During the day all the bedding was piled on the parental bed. Chests and trunks were unnecessary, as these people had only a few clothes, generally consisting of trousers and shirts for the menfolk, while the women dressed in homespun on weekdays and in calico on Sundays. The children ran around half naked. A few chairs roughly hewn and a big box which served as a table completed the household equipment. My friend Bill Taylor, his younger brother, and I spent our nights near a fine spring several yards from the cabin. Only a few acres of ground were tilled and planted with corn so as to provide the meal necessary for bread. The materials for their garments were woven and spun at home, and the other wants of these frugal people were supplied by hunting. They never troubled themselves about the future and were interested in nothing but where to catch the beavers most easily and where to find the greatest herds of buffalo. They paid no attention to the great stretches of the best arable soil, as there were no purchasers and the government had millions of other acres to give away.

During the next few days of my visit we made our preparations for the proposed buffalo hunt. A two-horse wagon was repaired. In order to keep the wagon cover taut in case of rain, wagon hoops of dogwood were provided. The nice long, straight, and sleek shoots

---

[1] Isaac (Ike) Russell Black was renowned in San Saba County for his hunting prowess. He was born in Meriwether County, Georgia, December 22, 1843. After residing at San Saba for a number of years, he moved to Everett, Washington, about 1900. See Jym A. Sloan, *Old Timers of Wallace Creek* (San Saba: privately printed, 1958), pp. 87–89.

chase all at the same time, each man selecting one and not more than two buffalo at which to fire. But if the herd ran toward our camp, we were to postpone shooting until we reached the vicinity of our camp, because the dead animals, skinned and quartered on the spot where they are killed, had to be loaded on our wagon and hauled to the camp. I was the last of the three of our party to reach the herd, which, when they discovered us, crowded into a mass and, led by the strongest bull, sought to escape. I singled out a young fat buffalo and kept galloping at his side, waiting for Taylor's shot, which was to be the signal for the rest of us to shoot. Being only a few yards ahead of me, he killed his buffalo with the first shot, but as I was using a six-shooter instead of a rifle, two shots were necessary to land my young heifer, while Bill had to shoot five times before he could bag his quota, which proved to be an old buffalo cow. All this happened while the herd was thundering on like a hurricane.

We did not kill any more that day but were kept busy trying to extricate ourselves and our horses from the turbulent mass which now had become deaf and blind from fright. When chasing wild steers in Texas we could see their heads with their fine, long horns in the air. But the buffalo would run with their heads lowered and covered by their long and dense manes, and there was great danger both to ourselves and our horses being gored by their wildly tossing horns. When we returned to the animals we had killed, we found that they lay half a mile apart.

People who have never taken part in similar hunts have no conception of the excitement which takes hold of the hunter. Even persons indifferent to hunting will have their blood set to tingling by this sport, sharing the excitement of both the hunter and the horse. When the chase extends over a distance of three to five miles, the herd scatters considerably, the stronger animals taking the lead while the weaker lag behind. When this happened with our herd, I made the singular observation, which I found in no other animal of gregarious habits—that the leaders, when tired out by a long run, alternated the use of their legs, placing the greatest weight on the right legs for a time, then changing to the left, which could be distinctly observed and was instantly imitated by the whole herd.

I communicated this fact to Colonel Theodore Roosevelt when

he came to San Antonio to organize his Rough Riders, and it made
such an impression on him that he made a note of it in order to use
it in one of his later hunting treatises. Too bad that Roosevelt did
not write more books! The Spanish-American War made him a
famous man, and after being elected by the Republican party to
the vice-presidency, he became president after McKinley's death.
Aside from his affable manners, it was his remarkable memory that
excited my admiration. Since he himself had led the life of a cowboy for several years on his ranch, there were many things we had
in common. It was a pet idea of his that every man should rear a
large family, as the care for numerous offspring would compel the
parents to be industrious and self-sacrificing. On one occasion
Colonel Roosevelt asked me for a picture of my family representing
the parents sitting amidst their twelve children, and when I promised to let him have the picture on his return from Cuba, he laugh-
ingly and in his good-natured way said: "All right, but then there
will be thirteen instead of twelve." I tried to defend myself by saying that I was superstitious about the number thirteen. But it was
six long years before I could send the picture to the White House,
where it was kept hanging for several years. Colonel Roosevelt acknowledged receipt of the picture in a friendly letter bearing this
postscript: "Are you still superstitious? I can discover only twelve
children in the picture."

It was too late to cut up the buffalo, so one of our boys returned
to the wagon for provisions, since we had to camp beside our game
to keep off the wolves. We opened up their arteries and bled them
profusely and removed their "innards." On the next morning our
wagon arrived and we hastily skinned the animals and disjointed
the beautiful horns. After quartering each animal we loaded the
meat on our wagon and transferred it to our camp. I now learned
how to cure and preserve buffalo meat. Our big kettle was filled
with water and a few handfuls of salt and nitre added. Large chunks
of solid meat free of bones and with tendons removed were sliced
into smooth pieces, whereupon the entire meat supply was gener-
ously rubbed with salt and nitre, the latter being an excellent means
of preserving the fine red color of the meat. The smaller pieces were
dipped in the boiling water for several minutes, which caused the
albumen of the raw meat to coagulate, after which they were sus-

pended from the branches of trees to be smoked. The larger pieces were treated somewhat differently. After having been impregnated with salt and nitre like the smaller slices, they were packed in a barrel and soaked in a strong brine, then later smoked. Buffalo meat treated in this way was a delicacy, and the larger pieces retained their fresh color for months provided the skin was removed. Within twelve days we killed twelve buffalo, and their hides, stretched and dried, in addition to the cured meat made a load of two thousand pounds for our wagon. So our hunting trip had been well worth all it had cost in time and trouble.

At nights on this hunting trip we frequently indulged in hunting that odd and singular creature called the armadillo. After our dogs had tracked them they could easily be caught on foot or with a cudgel. Their meat was useless, but from their hard and horny armature beautiful baskets could be made for the ladies. On this hunting trip we did not see or meet a single Indian, although a numerous party of them had been hunting on the same grounds just a week before. It is an odd fact and difficult to understand that the settlers of the wilderness, surrounded as they are on all sides by dangers, grow careless and unmindful of the perils which constantly threaten them. They acquire the habit of relying on the instinct of their horses, which are afraid of the red man. They grow wild at the approach of an Indian and try to break loose and run, warning their masters by a loud and far-sounding whinny. The dogs, too, scent the redskins for great distances.

During this trip I had the best opportunity to study and appreciate the sterling character qualities of my companions. They were frugal in the highest degree and so hospitable that they would share all they had with their friends and were ever ready to help those who needed assistance. Our old friend Taylor knew from long experience the medicinal herbs and their effect on the human body. Wild camomiles were used to counteract fever, the leaves of the senna plant to alleviate stomach troubles. Small wounds were cured by the application of mashed cactus leaves; deeper wounds were antiseptically treated by applying sugar, first melted, then pulverized, or by alum prepared in the same way. As there were no doctors in these parts, the settlers managed to get along without their help.

Everybody was content with his own property. There was no
envy, no grudge, because those who were well off were always ready
to share their bounty with the indigent. People without means wish-
ing to cultivate their little piece of land would borrow a plow from
one neighbor and a team from another. In cases of sickness all the
neighbors combined to do the work necessary on the farm of the
sick or afflicted.

Sunday was not celebrated very strictly. If there was an empty
log house suitable for religious worship, the neighbors met there to
hail one another and to exchange news and ideas. Someone would
read a few chapters from the Bible and all would join in singing old-
fashioned hymns. The young people amused themselves by showing
their skill in shooting, throwing the lasso, and in horse racing. Sometimes they practiced the art of throwing the tomahawk, an art now
forgotten and extinct long ago. The hatchets or short-handled axes
used for this kind of sport were thrown at trees about fifteen feet
away and had to embed themselves deep enough to remain in the
tree. Then there was the favorite pastime of the spelling match,
young and old, men, women, and children taking part in them. The
one best educated pronounced the words, while those who felt equal
to the task raised their hands and spelled away. It was amusing to
see little children spell down their parents and to notice the parental
pride when they were beaten by their youngsters.

During the time spent in our buffalo camp, which we changed
several times, the members of the Taylor family urged me to make
San Saba my future home because every young settler and every
rifle was a benefit to the community. At last I assented. We agreed
that I should return to Helena to settle my affairs and rejoin them
within a month. I decided to accompany my companions back to
Menard, where we separated, the Taylors going east to San Saba
while I traveled south in order to touch Mason, Fredericksburg,
Comfort, Boerne, and San Antonio on my return to Helena. I mention the first four little towns because they were German settlements and their inhabitants mostly Rhinelanders.

The German Settlements

AFTER the Texans had gained their independence from Mexico on the battlefield at San Jacinto, they established an independent republic which existed for ten years before Texas was annexed by the Union. To colonize a country of such enormous size ready money and settlers were needed. Immigrants were attracted to Texas by free land grants. Two enterprising Americans, Miller and Fisher, engaged in return for large grants of land near the Llano River to bring to Texas between two and three thousand immigrants and to settle them in this part of the country, which in those days was peopled largely by Indians. After many vain efforts in Ireland and other countries the two men entered an agreement with the "Mainzer Adels-Verein," by which the society agreed to bring a large number of German settlers to Texas. The president of the German society was Prince Solms-Braunfels, and they called themselves the "Union of Princes and Noblemen for the Protection of German Immigrants to Texas." The headquarters of the society was at the city of Mainz, and the gentlemen actually succeeded in inducing more than one thousand inhabitants of the little principality of Hesse-Nassau, peasants and mechanics, to join the adventurous expedition to Texas. An advance party of these emigrants was put on board small sailing vessels bound for Indianola, Texas, and after a passage of from six weeks to several months disembarked at that little port. These aristocratic gentlemen were very poor businessmen, as they failed to provide provisions sufficient for the sustenance of so large a number of people. The land to be colonized was more than three hundred miles from Indianola, and no transportation facilities had been provided for the journey northward. The newcomers compelled to camp out on the low, damp coast were attacked by cholera and malaria, and a great many died before they were able to leave the coast. The others had to help themselves as best they could and offered their services to American farmers in southern, eastern, and central Texas. Many remained in these parts after they had become used to their new environment and became the founders of the German settlements—Schulenburg, Weimar, and others.

After many delays the majority of the Rhinish immigrants arrived. A nobleman, Herr von Meusebach, had undertaken the management of this colony. The passengers with their families, totaling nearly two thousand, again disembarked at Indianola, but this time at least some provisions had been made for their convenience, especially oxcarts, although insufficient in numbers, were ready for their transportation into the interior. It soon became known that the land granted to the settlers was not likely to be settled for the time being, as it still was inhabited by Indians; then too, sufficient means were lacking to transport their belongings to their destination, a distance of more than three hundred miles. A part of these people therefore remained in Indianola and the other small towns in the neighborhood—Victoria, Yorktown, and Clinton—while the majority of them founded the town of New Braunfels about thirty miles northeast of San Antonio. During the first two years these settlers could hardly procure the bare necessities of life, their chief needs being seed, teams, and farming implements. Amidst great privations, however, they managed to overcome all these difficulties. The newcomers learned to raise corn and other crops suited to the climate. Eventually the land in the neighborhood was purchased and the city enlarged. Prince Solms-Braunfels came in person from his ancestral castle near the city of Limburg to inspect the town which had been named in his honor.

New Braunfels is situated at the foot of a mountain range belonging to the limestone formation, which gives rise to the Comal River, which through its rapid and abundant flow of water develops waterpower equal to four hundred horsepower. Today this power is used to supply three thousand inhabitants of the city with water and electric lights and to produce the power necessary to operate local flour mills and other industries established at New Braunfels.

Max Krueger, age sixteen, when departing from Germany in 1868.

Carl Erdman and Dorathea Bremer Kreuger, parents of Max.

Friedrich and Karoline Gerlach Buergener, parents of Emily Buergener Krueger.

Max Krueger (*right*) and his brother Carl at Helena in 1870.

The original of this picture, the only known example of Krueger's photographic career, bears the note "O Hotel in Borne [i.e., Boerne] 1874. Papa took it."

Left: The original of this photograph bears the imprint "M. Krueger, Photographer." He was twenty-four. *Right*: Emily Buergener Krueger at age twenty.

Krueger's home at Twin Sisters, about 1873.

The Krueger family in 1902. *Back row*: Wallie, Walter, Willy, Max, Paul, Dora, Lee; *front*: Carl, Mrs. Krueger with Marguerite, Pettye, Dixie, Krueger, and Alex. Krueger sent a copy of this picture to Theodore Roosevelt and for a time it hung in the White House.

March 7, 1904

Dear Mr. Krueger:

Accept for yourself and Mrs. Krueger, and especially for Mrs. Krueger, heartiest congratulations on your large nice family. I am proud of you both as good citizens and am delighted to have the photograph. I am very sorry that I have no picture of my family to send you in return.

With good wishes for you all,

Sincerely yours,

Theodore Roosevelt

Mr. M. Krueger
San Antonio Machine & Supply Co.,
San Antonio, Texas.

Krueger met Roosevelt when he was in San Antonio recruiting Rough Riders. Amazed to learn of Krueger's eleven children, Roosevelt asked for a picture when the family reached an even dozen.

Krueger later in life, with his sculptress.

Krueger's business card, San Antonio Machine and Supply Company.

In time a great many stragglers arrived from Indianola. These, with the surplus of the prolific German families, moved farther north and west in the direction of the Fisher and Miller colony once so ardently desired and so confidently promised. A great number of German families also settled in San Antonio; others stopped at Boerne and Comfort. In and around the latter town a party of immigrants from the university city of Freiburg had settled, among them several highly educated people and a few university professors. These gentlemen did some farming and stock-raising. The rapidly increasing towns of this region were provided with shingles split from cypress trees growing along the Guadalupe River and hauled to their destination in large oxcarts. There was a story circulating among the settlers that these Freiburg and Heidelberg professors had made a vow to give their descendants a thorough German education and therefore to talk only in Latin and Greek during the intervals of their hard work. We have reason to believe that this was only a joke told on them and that it came to be believed as happens with many stories of this kind.

The next German settlement to be founded was Fredericksburg, first built as one long, wide street along a most beautiful valley, situated seventeen hundred feet above sea-level. Its climate is cooler and consequently more agreeable than that of New Braunfels and, being midway between San Antonio and Llano County, at a distance of about seventy-five miles from the city just named, it now boasts of a population of nearly three thousand souls, most of whom are employed in tilling the soil.

The German immigrants have done much to disseminate a high degree of culture in Texas. Their farms are better and more intelligently worked than those of the average American and therefore yield better crops. Their houses, almost always surrounded by little flower gardens, are models of cleanliness; the majority of them are repainted at frequent intervals, and they look like neat play-houses. Schools and churches are provided and are well attended, but their jails are empty, as few crimes are committed among the Germans, nearly all of whom are in comfortable financial circumstances. A part of their wealth is accounted for by the favorable location of all their little towns, lying along the great commercial routes that led from the coast to the many military posts which dotted the country at that time. These stations had been established by the government for the protection of the colonists from the encroachments of hostile Indians and were an excellent means of fostering commercial intercourse in those parts.

My next stopping place before reaching Helena was San Antonio, which today is one of the finest cities in America. At the time of my visit it was beginning slowly to develop from a dirty Mexican village into a modern American city. More than two hundred years ago Spanish Franciscan monks had established a chain of five missions, employing for this purpose the native Indians after their conversion to the Christian faith. These missions contained homes for the converted Indians, a church, school, granaries, and storehouses. The city and the missions just mentioned were all built along the banks of the San Antonio River, the springs of which rise at the foot of the hills only a few miles away. Irrigation ditches many miles long bear witness to the experience, skill, and knowledge of these enterprising monks. Each mission was enclosed by a high stone wall and regularly fortified and garrisoned so as to withstand the attacks of hostile Indians. One of these missions is the famous Alamo, also called the "Thermopylae of America." It was there that in the War for Texas Independence (1835–36) 183 Americans fought a Mexican army of 3,000 men under the command of General Santa Anna. After a long and heroic resistance the small band of defenders was overpowered and massacred, but not before 700 Mexicans had paid with their lives for it. Of this fact we are reminded by the historical and classic saying known all over Texas: "Thermopylae had her messenger of defeat; the Alamo had none."

The principal thoroughfare of San Antonio presented a lively aspect in these early times. This city was the trade center for all the goods freighted on oxcarts from the coast to all parts of the interior. A very active and profitable trade was also carried on with Mexico. The goods arriving from or destined for Mexico were usually transported by large, two-wheeled carretas. As a matter of course San Antonio still looked entirely Mexican. The language universally heard and spoken was Spanish, and indeed the Mexican part of San Antonio's population was of a type to be proud of, as the king of Spain had settled in the city two hundred prominent families from the Canary Islands.

Of special interest to the stranger were the Spanish costumes. The señoras and señoritas were mostly dressed in black and covered their hair with the familiar mantilla. Unlike the Texas cowboys, the rancheros, owners of the great pastures on the Rio Grande, spent a great part of their wealth for their costumes. An important part of the Mexican costume was the sombrero, the well-known Mexican hat, which was embroidered all over with silver or gold thread in exquisite patterns and wires of precious metals. The coat-of-arms of Mexico, representing the Mexican eagle carrying a snake in its talons, was an almost indispensable part of each sombrero. In like manner the black velvet coats were covered with embroideries. The spurs of these Mexican gentlemen used to be of silver and of extraordinary size. Splendid also were the trappings of the saddle horses. The buckles of the bridle reins were generally chased, the reins braided of many tinted horsehairs and amply provided with tassels of the same colors and materials. The shape of the Mexican saddles was different from that of the Texas saddles, and the caparisons used with them were covered with expensive embroideries. All the greater was the constant contrast presented by the peons, the peasant class of Mexico, people living in the greatest poverty and working for wages that were next to nothing or making a living by begging and treated no better than slaves.

During the night the Mexicans attended dances and indulged in drinking, and their fandango or national dances were sights worth seeing. All over the city until late at night strains of music could be heard, as bands of musicians used to go from house to house playing their tunes for a small compensation, while in the more stylish quarters of the city young gentlemen serenaded their lady-loves. A guitar adorned with many silk ribbons was to be found in every Mexican home. At the approach of evening the señoritas dressed in white and adorned themselves with flowers and ribbons, but the windows of their rooms were furnished with lattice-work of heavy iron bars which impeded any personal contact with their lovers beyond a bashful kiss or shake of the hand.

The poor people amused themselves on the public plazas provided with tables and illuminated by great lanterns, where Mexican dishes and beverages were served by pretty black-eyed girls. The most delicious of those dishes was chile con carne, literally "red pepper with meat." As the name of the dish implies, it was very peppery, the meat being in the minority. Tamales are a favorite dish in San Antonio even at the present time. They consist of any kind of meat, chopped very fine, rolled in meal, and covered with cornshucks. They should be eaten while hot. Tortillas are thin flat cakes made of cornmeal that is prepared after this fashion: the cornseed are saturated with a strong solution of lye until they have swelled considerably; then they are ground to a mush between two rounds of stones and baked in a pan like pancakes. Frijoles (Mexican beans) and very strong hot Mexican coffee made what is supposed to be a "square meal." Gambling dens and vaudeville theatres were open day and night, and it was interesting to note how great heaps of silver and Mexican and American gold changed hands across the gambling tables. The players had huge stacks of cash money lying in front of them. Paper money was not in use in those resorts.

The trade of the city was carried on chiefly by Germans and Americans, but there was scarcely any social intercourse between the different races, the Germans living on adjoining streets, the Mexicans in the center of the city near the plazas, and the Americans in the beautiful neighborhood of the military post. The Negroes, who were fairly numerous and almost as filthy as the poor Mexicans, had their huts and small houses in the northern part of the city. Having been delivered from slavery by emancipation only a few years before, they were peaceful and industrious and easily handled. The Germans living in their respective settlements generally confined their intercourse to their own compatriots and did not take part in any except local politics. They kept true to their native virtues and faults. Among the latter I would say the worst was their discord and paltry jealousy of such of their countrymen as were more successful in business or unable to get used to their narrow way of thinking and acting. Very often the thought struck me what a powerful factor the Germans could be in American affairs if they would take an active part in national politics and cast a united vote like the Irish. They would be more esteemed as a whole and in all probability could have kept the United States out of the World War.

Henderson's Ranch

MY journey's end was now at hand and I reached Helena one week after my departure from Mr. Taylor's home in Menard. I was still determined to spend the coming years in beautiful San Saba, and only a few days were required in making my preparation to return. I exchanged the horse I had left in Helena for a so-called Henry rifle, a rifle just invented which had to be loaded with cartridges and which, in spite of its small caliber, was a powerful weapon of great accuracy of aim in the hands of a good marksman. Nothing particular had happened in the little town during my absence— only some of the worst gun-toters had been removed by the soldiers. *Arriving in Yorktown, where I had no welcome offered to me, I at once made arrangements to move with Emily to San Saba. Having scant means, we could only hire a wagon to take us as far as Bell County, where for a short time I helped to make saddletrees for a man named Bidwell. Finally we arrived at Henderson's Ranch, fifteen miles above San Saba town, where we remained nearly a year.*

I spent an entire week with my hospitable hunting companions, busy hunting deer and fishing. We dressed the deerskins, and our most disagreeable task was to move them after they had been treated with deers' tallow. Fishing was easier and much more pleasant. We stretched a thin rope across the river so it would not touch the surface of the water. To this rope we tied twenty short fishing lines at equal distances. The entire contrivance was put out every evening and inspected every morning, and it was easy to ascertain which of the baited hooks had been taken, for the captured fish tried to escape as we approached and pulled in our lines. As there was no market for fish, we caught only what we needed for dinner, throwing the others back into the water. Some people tried to make use of the superabundance of the fish by feeding them to their hogs, but the experiment failed on account of the fish bones. Besides fish the river contained many turtles, which liked to bask on the rocks rising above the water. We dared not shoot them through the body, as holes in the shell would have decreased the value, so they had to be shot through the head, and the hunter had to wade into the water to secure his game. While doing this one day I noticed at the bottom of the river thousands of clams with their sharp sides turned upward, and I sustained a severe injury to my foot by stepping on one of them. Opening some of them in order to use the flesh for fishbait, I discovered the first beautiful specimen of freshwater pearl. Later I spent many a Sunday afternoon in pearl hunting, and after half a year's work I was the owner of several hundred small and medium-sized pearls which I subsequently sold in Europe. It was necessary to be very patient in this task, for frequently a hundred clams had to be opened before a single small pearl of value could be found, while it required thousands of clams to find one really valuable pearl.

I was now a young man of nineteen, and I had begun to see that this kind of life would not suit me as a career. I made up my mind to look for regular, well-paying employment, and as I still had both of my fine horses, I determined to work again as a cowboy. I found employment with Messrs. Murray and Montgomery and was told to be ready to assist in moving a herd of cattle to Kansas. But, as so often in my life, a disagreeable accident frustrated my plans. After my return to Taylor's home in the evening I had hobbled my tired horses and turned them out to graze. When I went to look for them before retiring, they were nowhere to be found. I went in search of them at early dawn and from the top of a hill heard and saw horses being chased by Indians in the direction of Cherokee Creek. I ran to Taylor's house in all haste, but they had already been notified that during the night the Comanches had stolen nearly two-thirds of all the horses in the settlement, my own included.

The horses of the Taylors were already saddled, and after they had given me one of theirs we hastened to join the pursuers who had gathered at Henderson's place. We took only a scanty supply of provisions, just enough to last us for a day. When Henderson, an old Indian guide himself, had taken command of our party consisting of fifteen men, we broke up into three sections, to follow, if possible, the tracks of the stolen horses to the point where the different troops of the Indians combined.[1] As the grass was still wet, we could see the tracks plainly and followed them in the greatest haste for half an hour, or until the sun rising higher and higher absorbed the dew and pursuit became more difficult. About seven miles above Henderson's Ranch at a ford on the San Saba River, all the tracks merged and we found that the number of stolen horses amounted to about forty and that they were driven by at least a dozen Indians. We had already lost much time in our efforts to recover our horses and did not reach the ford until noon. We rested our horses for an hour, had lunch, and took up the chase once more. The redskins had outdistanced us considerably. Still, we gained on them, and toward evening when we were compelled to camp for the night they were only six miles away. We mounted our horses at dawn the next day and an hour later reached the place where the Comanches had passed the night. We did not find any traces of a campfire, but we discovered that they had killed a colt and eaten its hindquarters.

The pursuit now became difficult because we came to a region covered with thick underbrush, and only narrow trails that were barely passable by an individual led across this hilly brushwood. The Comanches, experiencing great difficulty in getting horses through these narrow trails, split again into small groups in order

[1] James Elias Henderson settled in San Saba County in 1854. Born in Tennessee on August 7, 1808, he emigrated to Texas and was in Bastrop County by 1832. He served a year in the Texas army, beginning December 14, 1836, and from time to time served with the Texas Rangers. He was wounded in the Battle of Plum Creek and received 1,280 acres of land for his service. Henderson married Martha Flint on September 12, 1842, and they had eight children. Their great-grandsons, Frank and Thomas A. Sloan, still ranch in the area where Krueger knew Henderson, and the remains of the mill Krueger operated for Henderson are still discernable. Henderson died March 30, 1883. See Jym A. Sloan, *Old Timers of Wallace Creek* (San Saba: privately printed, 1958), pp. 55–72; and Thomas Lloyd Miller, *Bounty and Donation Land Grants in Texas* (Austin and London: The University of Texas Press, 1967), p. 338. Jym A. Sloan was Henderson's grandson.

to reach the Bald Mountains, a chain of thickly wooded hills. Our old friend Henderson, having passed all his life in these wilds, had acquired a keen perception of the ways of the wilderness almost akin to the instincts of a wild animal. He now saw an opportunity to get even with the Indians. We were at that moment rather close to them, only a half-mile space separating us, when we noticed that the larger troop of redskins with many of our horses tried to gain the summit of the hill by making a circuitous route through a more open part of the country. Their idea was to shoot us as we were making our way through the maze of thicket. Since no shot was fired, we concluded that they had no other arms than bows and arrows and could not be very dangerous. So we began the attack by firing in dead earnest. The Indians tried for some minutes to keep the horses together, but they soon lost control and the frightened animals stampeded in all directions. They dismounted in mad haste, and their horses, becoming excited by the din of combat, broke loose and joined the herd which we had previously rescued. Further pursuit was now out of the question, as the Indians were able to hide in the most inaccessible places while we, who were on our horses, could not hope to follow. We were forty miles from the nearest settlement and our rations were short, so we concluded that the sensible thing to do would be to round up our horses and start for home. Sheer hunger compelled us to shoot a calf, which we had for supper, and then we made camp for the night. Half of our boys had to watch the horses till midnight, while others of us took our turn at guarding till morning. With the dawn of day we returned to our homes without any trouble.

During the pursuit we had seen many bloody tracks, caused probably by our own horses, three of which had been wounded by our own shots. But we did not find any dead Indians. When an Indian is shot his comrades, even at the risk of their own lives, will drag his body to safety whether dead or alive. In a series of fights with Indians, as well as the encounter just described, we seldom found the body of a dead Indian, but a few days later we found several and they were all buried according to Indian custom; that is, the bodies had been deposited on the summit of a hill and covered with heavy rocks to keep the wolves away. Frequently we would find the quiver and bow of the dead warrior beside the body.

About fifteen miles from Henderson's Ranch we met three of our neighbors who brought us some provisions. They had followed our tracks, and the bacon, bread, and coffee they brought us tasted delicious. They told us that thirty-six horses had been stolen, but since we recovered thirty-one, our loss was relatively small. Unfortunately my two horses, which were my only earthly possessions besides my weapons, were among the few horses lost, and being deprived of them, I was unable to make the trip to Kansas with Murray and Montgomery.

At Henderson's Ranch I had an opportunity to get acquainted with a thoroughly different type of American. Old Mr. Henderson had passed his life as a scout and frontiersman until his fortieth year, when he was married to the daughter of an old Kentucky hunter who had settled in Texas very early, and when his first child was born he felt duty bound to provide sufficiently for his own offspring and to leave them in easy circumstances. When he left the government service, he was granted 320 acres which he could select wherever he pleased, and he selected the land near the San Saba River which was afterward known among the settlers as Henderson's Ranch. On the south bank of the river there was a rich valley of 160 acres covered with a luxurious growth of fine hardwood trees, principally water elms, pecan trees, poplars, and burr oaks. At first Mr. Henderson managed to supply his necessary means from the proceeds of a small herd of cattle. But every year a few more acres of the valley were cleared and made tillable by chopping down the trees and digging out and burning the stumps. Great harvests from this alluvial soil of the valley were his reward. Especially corn, wheat, sweet potatoes, and a variety of fruits and vegetables grew in abundance. South of the valley at the foot of a hill big springs gushed forth and irrigated the land. The rich crops gathered were sold at high prices and they were easily accessible to the government military posts. Mr. Henderson was soon in easy circumstances, and when other settlers adopted his methods this little settlement soon became the granary of the government stations. Yet, while the revenues from harvest and livestock increased, these people had to deny themselves many of the commodities of civilization. There were no railroads at that time and everything had to be hauled over poor roads from the coast three hundred miles away. There were no mills to grind wheat and corn, and the grain had to be ground on small handmills, the same as coffee. Almost all the houses were cabins constructed of logs and there were no planks for floors, window-frames, or doors.

Many years before my time Mr. Henderson had ordered a small sawmill, which was to be driven by the power from the springs near his ranch home, but when it arrived and was installed in primitive fashion, the waterpower proved to be insufficient, as the small dam constructed of loose rocks could not raise the surface of the water sufficiently to produce the required force. So I began to study the problem: how everything could be arranged to get the machinery in working order and derive from the mill the desired profit. This mental activity helped me to get over the loss of my horses, and my regrets for not being able to continue as a cowboy gradually diminished.

I entered Mr. Henderson's services for the space of three months. *Henderson gave us a small one-room block house without floor or windows. My work consisted of field work at fifty cents a day. Our furniture consisted of a dry goods box for a table, two Hostetter bitters boxes as seats, an iron skillet for baking cornbread, a coffee pot, and some tin plates and cups. With an old wood axe I had cut out the frame of a bedstead, with rawhide strings for a bottom and a sack of cornshucks for bedding. Our outside possession was a lame horse by the name of Spot, which the Indians soon stole. On Sundays I drove in a few wild cows, which we broke to milking.*

My first work was plowing with an ox team. As the soil was still full of roots, it required great efforts to make a straight furrow with one of these crude hand-made plows in use at the time, which were drawn by four or six yoke of oxen and required the services of two men, one to hold and direct the plow while the other urged the obstinate steers on with a whip fourteen feet long attached to an eight foot handle. The crack of these whips equalled the report of a gun, and as they were plaited with straps of rawhide, many blows left bloody scars. After eight days' work I had learned how to handle such a large team, and after one more week I was able to make straight furrows with the giant plow. I may state here that this is the hardest kind of work I know of. There is no need of a narcotic for the farmhand, who sinks down to his rest immediately after supper, and many loud calls and divers jabs in the ribs are necessary to rouse him the next morning. The other kinds of farm work were easier. Harrowing was done with a single or double yoke of oxen; planting, with horses. My excellent eyesight helped me greatly in sowing wheat, and I was very proud when the grain I had sown grew up uniformly. The neighbors too were glad to secure my services for this kind of work.

I have stated I had racked my brain for some weeks to find out how to use the sawmill to advantage, and I finally prevailed on Mr. Henderson to trust me with the work and to place at my disposal the help needed to complete the plant. My plan was to rebuild the dam from its foundations and to raise it ten feet higher than the original in order to increase its power. Cement, which would have been ideal material for such work, was of course not to be thought of. The former builders had used nothing but clay for this kind of masonry, but it was softened and constantly washed away from between the rocks by the pressure of the water. No other material except a good, hydraulic lime could be used, and as this could not be bought, I was compelled to produce it myself. My very first trial succeeded beyond my fondest hopes. On the flat ground I arranged a ten-foot square made of logs of mountain cedar about three feet thick. On these I deposited a two-foot layer of blue-gray limestone, alternating with a layer of cedar logs until the structure attained a height of fourteen feet. I then set it on fire, and as mountain cedar develops the greatest heat of any kind of wood, the limestone crumbled in the raging flame as readily as if it had been treated in a regular lime-kiln. To avoid admixture with the ashes, I placed the largest piece of fuel on the ground, and during the process of burning the air current assisted my purpose by blowing the light ashes from the top layers. After the entire pyramid had been burned and cooled down, I took a sample of the material and mixed it with the sharp granite sand found in the neighborhood. The result was very satisfactory, as I now had a satisfactory lime. In the meantime the necessary sand had been provided, together with flat rocks suitable for building and found in symmetrical layers nearby. Thus in a few weeks our work was finished. Ever since that time log cabins ceased to be built, and as building rocks were plentiful and everybody could use his own lime, regular chimneys and many rock houses were built.

Our next and greatest difficulty was the construction of the great overshot waterwheel. We made it from cypress boards, as they do not decay easily in water. Cypress trees could be found everywhere near the river, but the boards we had to saw by hand. After we had started with our construction work, the entire settlement took a lively interest in it, and everybody assisted us to the best of his ability, some working on the mill dam, others helping in the construction of the waterwheel, while still others made the flumes to be used in conducting the water current to the wheel. At the same time the sawmill machinery was installed. While all this was going on I had employed others to haul the logs we were to use, and as I did not know what kind of wood was best suited for boards and planks, I tried cedar, poplar, oak, and walnut. After three months of hard work we were able to produce the first boards, and soon the screeching noise of the circular saw could be heard daily throughout the resounding valleys, and we could deliver to the settlers all the straight boards they needed.

Emily and I were now able to buy some real furniture and bedding and moved into another block house close to the mill. A blizzard overtook us, and the chimney not being completed and having large cracks between the logs of the walls, our room was soon covered with snow and ice. A few days before, I had killed a hog and had hung the hams close to the bed, to be smoked by the unfinished chimney. Since we could not keep warm in the scanty clothes we called our own, we had to retire to bed and remain until the weather moderated. Our meals consisted of parts of the frozen hams, of which I cut the necessary slices with a hatchet.

Our neighbors now insisted that we should add a mill for grinding cornmeal to our little plant, and when we learned that a second-hand mill could be had somewhere below Austin, we purchased it for a small sum and added it to our equipment. Our establishment prospered and the neighbors soon began to supply their own logs, and we cut them for half of the boards, for which there was a good market. For grinding corn we received a toll of one-quarter of the meal.

My wages increased with the profits afforded by my work, and soon I was able to buy a fine horse and found leisure in which to go hunting occasionally. My constant companion on these hunting trips was Jim, Mr. Taylor's eldest son. The Indians now paid us a visit with every full moon and we had to fight out many a skirmish with them. As I have minutely described one of them, I shall not dwell on any more. While the maintenance of home and family in the wilderness very often necessitates the risk of life and limb, we youngsters not infrequently jeopardized both for sheer exuberance of spirit. I will relate here one instance.

One cold winter night Jim Taylor and I rode to Brady Creek to hunt wild turkeys, which were plentiful in those days. In the fall and winter their food consisted of the acorns and nuts that covered the ground in great quantities; during the summertime they fed on the seeds of various grasses and all sorts of berries. As they rarely ever suffered from lack of food, the gobblers attained a weight of thirty pounds and the hens twenty pounds. Their meat was white and tender and tasted delicious, and the oil produced by heating their fat served many and various purposes. During the day they were generally hunted by riding into their favorite haunts, dismounting, and hiding in the brush. With a turkey whistle made of bone the call of the turkey hens could be accurately imitated. Early in the morning when everything was quiet and not a leaf stirring, the gobblers would hear this call for almost half a mile and would soon answer it by a loud gobble. Turkey gobblers happen to be exceedingly jealous creatures. By their gobble they draw other gobblers to the scene, and many a tussle is fought between them on their way to the hunter's hiding place, so they actually sometimes seem to compete as to which shall be the first victim. Another way was to hunt the fat gobblers on horseback, as they soon tired out. At first they would rise in the air and not settle down again until they had flown several hundred yards, but soon the strength of their wings was exhausted and the birds would be compelled to use their legs as a means of escape. Naturally this kind of hunt requires an open country, as the birds are hard to catch in the underbrush and there must be a few trees where they can seek shelter. When the birds have once been "treed," they are a sure prey of the hunter. I sometimes chased a turkey for miles, and when it began to tire I dismounted and caught it on foot. But the finest way of catching turkeys is to hunt them during a moonlight night. They are then roosting on high trees, if possible, near some watercourse. I have noticed that they prefer smooth-barked trees, as the branches are more comfortable for their feet than the rough-barked ones. They are especially fond of roosting on cottonwood trees on account of their wide-spreading branches.

The moon was shining particularly bright the night Jim and I were on our way to Brady Creek, seven miles away, to get a few fat gobblers for our Sunday dinner. We could see almost as well as in the daylight. Tying our horses to a bush, we strained our ears to find out from what particular tree the first warning call of the turkeys was to come. We soon discovered a cottonwood tree on which nearly a dozen turkeys were roosting. Carefully avoiding every noise, we crept nearer. Sometimes dry branches cracked under our feet, and this roused all the birds from their sleep. Knowing that they would all fly the next moment, we both blazed away at the same time, bringing down two gobblers and one hen. For those night hunts we used the Enfield rifles loaded with buckshot which scattered widely at the discharge and sometimes killed several birds at a single shot. The hen we left untouched. Jim caught hold of the legs of one of the gobblers, while mine made a last effort and fluttered into the river nearby. As I had noticed that it was an especially fine specimen, I was unwilling to lose it, and, hastening to my saddle, I took my lasso and ran down the river, the swift current of which threatened to carry my game away. But before I could rope my bird, we heard a noise on the other side of the river as if some one were cautiously creeping over the ground to get near the river. We listened sharply, expecting Indians, and indeed, we heard the hooting of the screech-owl after a few moments, which was instantly answered from two other directions. The Comanches always used this sign at night as a means of communication, and, being sure that they had spied us, we darted back to our horses and made good our escape.

But we ran into another more dangerous situation. To get home to Henderson's Ranch we had to ride a distance of about eight miles. The only house to be met with on our way, close to our road, belonged to a Mr. Woods, a former sheriff. When within about a hundred yards of this house, Jim conceived the childish idea of trying to frighten Mr. Woods. He put spurs to his horse and let out a Comanche war-whoop resounding like a siren call among the hills. I lagged a little behind to tighten my saddle straps and awaited developments—a few shots from Woods' gun—and as it was too late for me to retreat, I followed Jim as fast as my horse could run. Just as I approached the house two shots were fired at me simultaneously, and the entire charge of buckshot lodged in a tree just a few feet in front of me. We now galloped home with our lone turkey which Jim had strapped to his saddle, but we could not withstand the temptation to return the next morning and jolly Mr. Woods about his poor marksmanship.

Here is the story Sheriff Woods told us. He with his brother-in-law had been watching their horses all night, for they had been informed of a recent horse raid by the Comanches. About midnight two redskins had sped past their house, yelling their war-whoop, and they had taken a shot at one of the Indians and were pretty sure one of their shots had taken effect, though they could not discover any signs of blood anywhere. They led us to the tree to admire the shot which was deeply imbedded in the wood, covering a space several inches wide, but we took good care not to let them know who the "Indians" were they had fired on, as they would never have believed it.

Pioneer Ways

THE little corn- and sawmills rendered a real service to all the families of the community. These people had settled here years before I arrived and had planted fruit trees and made other permanent improvements. One evening while sitting around the fireplace at Mr. Henderson's home we enumerated all the different varieties of plants that had been planted and had prospered, and found that we could grow all the necessities of life except coffee, whereupon we decided to give a banquet, the menu of which was to be composed entirely of those things with which kind Mother Nature had provided us so lavishly, and to invite all the neighbors within a radius of ten miles to participate. We made long tables of boards and benches designed to accommodate a hundred guests. Every guest had to bring his own plate, knife, fork, spoon, etc. Our neighbors helped in cooking, and the boys had to supply the kitchen with antelope and turkeys, while the girls caught fish in the nearby river. The tables were decorated with beautiful wildflowers, and they nearly broke under the weight of all the homegrown delicacies served upon them. The flour of our fine wheat was turned into bread, cakes, and pies; our gardens provided a great variety of vegetables, including cauliflower. Game, fowl, fresh and preserved fruit, wild honey in place of sugar, whipped cream, turtle soup, and many other delicacies were in abundance.

We were proud to have provided all these things by our own labor and exertions. Never in all my life have I seen people so happy; never have I felt so content and at home as among those simple people, the majority of whom had no better than a very primitive and superficial education. Some of them could not even write their names, and when a contract or other legal document was to be signed, they would make their "mark," which in turn was certified by those who were better educated.

A virtue truly beautiful was the great hospitality practiced everywhere by everybody. Never under any circumstances was money accepted for a night's lodging or even for a longer stay at any house. It did happen once, but it was my own fault and the money was refunded. One evening when Old Mr. Henderson and I returned home after a hard day's work, a light carriage stopped before our house, the owner and driver asking for lodging for himself and companion. They were welcomed into the home, and I helped unhitch the horses while Jim fed them. The strangers entered the house and immediately occupied the two rocking-chairs in front of the fireplace, which were the seats of honor for the old people. Mrs. Henderson—a grand old lady—asked the two men if they had any particular wishes for their supper, or if they would be content with our simple fare. People living in the solitude of nature are always modest, but these gentlemen wanted roast chicken, and the daughter of the house prepared it for them. I was aggravated by their insolent behavior and lost my temper entirely next morning when Jim and I were ordered to curry and feed their horses and to grease the axles of their carriage, so we agreed to charge these haughty fellows two dollars for their lodging. The two dollars were paid, but Jim took charge of the money, and instead of handing it over to his parents at the time, he kept it for awhile. But the senior Henderson felt uncomfortable with those two dollars in his pockets, so we had to get in our light wagon and follow the strangers. We caught up with them after a twelve-mile drive and returned the money.

From time to time more settlers arrived and brought with them many commodities which we had been deprived of for a long time. Many of the newcomers brought furniture, some of them cooking stoves, pots, and other kitchen utensils. Slowly the tin plates and cups vanished from the tables to be replaced by chinaware. A schoolhouse was built and it was used for religious worship as well. A teacher was appointed, but it was a long time before a preacher could be procured.

The little town of San Saba, fifteen miles away, slowly increased. The establishment of a drug store, managed by Dr. Rogan, was a valuable addition to our community, for the doctor soon began to give medical advice and treat patients.[1] Letters and newspapers had to be hauled on horseback over a distance of fifteen miles, and the settlers took their turns in rendering this service. We were glad when a man by the name of Harley began to trade in hardware and implements because these were the things most sorely needed. There were also some simple pieces of furniture ordered from Austin for such people as could afford these luxuries.

Another homemade substance was soap, and every settler manufactured this for himself in the following way: a good-sized woodbox was changed into an inverted pyramid, the top part of which was wider than the bottom, which formed a point. This pyramidal box was filled with fresh wood ashes, preferably of oak wood. On top of the pyramid a barrel was placed and its bunghole opened to permit the water to drip into and permeate the ashes. A little trough at the lower end conducted the lye from the barrel into a keg directly into an iron kettle. It was then heated and, after one added the required quantity of salt, bacon rinds, and other fatty refuse of the kitchen or tallow or fat, was boiled for three hours. During the process of cooling all impurities settled at the bottom of the kettle, the pure soap hardened, was taken from the kettle, cut into pieces, and put away for future use. This was a good soap but very caustic and suitable for laundry purposes only. Vinegar was made by using the berries of the sumac plant, soaking them in water during the night, filtering the water from the berries, and placing it in large jars.

Those hardy pioneers were long-lived. Deaths were very rare even in serious cases like typhoid fever. We let nature have its course and aided it with home remedies. In cases of serious wounds we would, of course, have preferred the service of a surgeon, but as this was impossible, someone who had had experience in such matters had to undertake the treatment and assume the risk. My first

[1] Dr. J. C. Rogan was one of the founders of the town of San Saba in 1854 (Alma Ward Hamrick, "Forty Years of Pioneers in San Saba County, 1846–1886," *West Texas Historical Association Yearbook* 11 [1935]: 13).

experience in this line I had in the corn mill. Ike Miller, a well-behaved, quiet man who took my place when some other task required my temporary absence, had the misfortune to fall into the cogwheel which was coupled to our waterwheel, and was carried into the gearing. I was startled by the sudden stop of the machine and, returning to the plant, found Miller with one arm broken, one hand entirely crushed, and three of his toes off. As all the members of the Henderson family were absent except the womenfolk, and I could not leave the wounded man unattended, I first asked the advice of Mrs. Henderson and then went to work cutting the boot from the injured leg and then with the same knife amputated the three toes which dangled from shreds of skin. I cleansed the wounds with soap and water and dressed them with cloth patches soaked in turpentine. In a similar though more cautious way I treated his hand, which was in a bad condition indeed. I put the broken arm in a splint with pieces of board in order to have the bones grow back straight together. During the process of healing some minor complications set in, but I treated these with sugar and alum. After a week's time Dr. Rogan arrived and examined the wounds but did not make any change in the treatment, leaving the situation in my hands. The healing process continued fast and satisfactorily, and after this experience my services were in greater demand than was convenient for me.

As time passed I became enamored of farm work. I had been told by a Mexican that in El Paso onions grew as large as saucers, transparent like crystal, and almost as sweet as apples. El Paso was five hundred miles away and we had no communication of any description with that city. After many delays and disappointments I succeeded in getting some of the onion seed, which I carefully planted. The onions grew splendidly and contained all the qualities mentioned, except they did not taste like apples but like onions, although the mild variety. Unfortunately the culture of onions did not bring us any financial returns, because we had no connection with the cities and onions were unsuited for transportation over long roads. Besides, there were wild onions growing everywhere. In later years the growing of onions proved to be a very profitable industry. The Bermuda onion has been responsible for the prosperity of extensive districts. Laredo and the Rio Grande Valley country annually ship thousands of carloads to the markets of the North and East, and the industry is rapidly advancing.

Like the American bison, generally called buffalo, which has been largely exterminated by human greed, a great many other kinds of animals have vanished from the American soil, save a few specimens kept in zoological gardens. The clever beaver and the graceful antelope have also been practically exterminated. The same fate has overtaken many kinds of beautiful birds, namely, the bird-of-paradise and wild pigeon. I watched one of the last great flights of these birds on their migrations from the north to the south. In the fall of the year when the cedar berries were ripe the first flocks appeared on the San Saba River. They came in such droves that they could not find roosting room on the trees. The stragglers sometimes arrived in flocks that darkened the sun for a few minutes at a time. They established headquarters in the cedar forests so often mentioned, because the cedar berries supplied them with a copious amount of food.

At such times every man who was able to carry a gun, afoot, on horseback, or in a wagon, betook himself to these woods, and for many weeks nothing could be heard but the report of guns. Thousands of innocent creatures were wantonly killed, because some were unfit for table use, as the berries on which they lived had a strong flavor of turpentine, thus spoiling the taste of the meat. A still harder fate awaited the poor birds in the springtime when they began nesting instead of returning north. The farmers, being afraid that the pigeons were going to ruin their crops, decided to burn the beautiful cedar forests. For weeks and even months the sky was black with clouds of smoke and the fine particles of ashes carried along by the wind would settle in the lungs and make breathing difficult and painful. In this way some of the most profitable forests of mountain cedar in our state were forever destroyed.

We had now accustomed ourselves to a life of regular work, toilsome indeed but affording many comforts. Only on bright moonlight nights did we experience much unrest and anxiety. Our log cabin was not far from the river crossing used regularly by the Comanches to pass into the San Saba valley on their murderous and pilfering expeditions among the settlements. Sometimes in small gangs, sometimes in great detachments, they passed our house, which of course we kept carefully closed and barricaded. Occasionally they would cut down our corn and pelt our roofs with stones and when they felt entirely secure would utter their wild warwhoop. We would take positions near the small crevices and prepare ourselves for defense with rifle and six-shooter, impatiently waiting for the dawn of day. Frequently on their roving expeditions the Comanches would have some of their women accompany them on foot, using them instead of packhorses and loading them with dried meat and blankets, while they, the leaders, would ride along with no other load but their weapons.

My last experience was in August, 1871. To assist a sick neighbor, N. King, I hauled a load of peaches with a yoke of steers to San Saba for him. I arrived there at night and camped on the south side of the small frame building used as a courthouse, so that I might be protected from the first norther that had sprung up. About midnight a severe storm set in, blowing the house down. Most of the timber blew over me, without leaving so much as a scratch, but one of my work steers became badly crippled. At daybreak several horsemen passed me, telling that a large band of Comanches had swooped down on our settlement and that all the horses had been stolen. Their object was to organize a posse in the town to follow the Indians. I had left Emily alone in the block house and our little home was the most exposed one. It was impossible to get a horse, so I undertook to run back home on foot, choosing mountain trails where I was fairly safe, but the heavy brogans blistered my feet fearfully. On reaching the house, I found the yard full of Indian tracks and feared Emily had been taken captive. I chased down to the next neighbors, Taylor and Black, but no one had seen a trace of her. Everyone preparing for a chase of the redskins, I now went to the Hendersons, my last hope to find Emily. The horses were saddled and guns and provisions gotten ready to overtake our enemy. I mounted with the others, but just as we were leaving I heard the joyous news that Emily had spent the night with the Sloan family and was safe, not even knowing of her close escape.

With the growing population of these sections the raids of the Indians became less frequent. Many of the farmers had built comfortable houses for themselves and provided them with doors and windows, using their old log cabins for barns. The better breeds of horses were protected at night by thick iron ox-chains stretched across the doors of their stables, but sometimes this contrivance did not prove effective, for the reason that the horse thieves would tie the horses' legs and drag them flat on the ground into the open. Failing in this, they usually killed the horses with arrows to get revenge on the owners. From time to time children were kidnapped and dragged into captivity. When half grown, the girls would become the wives of Indian chiefs, while the boys, instructed in all the arts and wiles of the redskins, soon forgot their parents and even their mother tongue. Such captives, when rescued and returned to their homes and relatives, never felt happy among civilized people and in some instances would even try to escape at the first opportunity. A typical case of this kind was a German boy who had been kidnapped near Fredericksburg when he was five years old and who lived among the Indians for sixteen years. He was rescued by a company of frontiersmen after a furious fight and returned to Fredericksburg, where his relatives managed to keep him for four years before he became accustomed to the usual routine farm work and to speaking the German language. But when a band of ravaging and murderous Comanches invaded the country, he disappeared with them. In later years he was said to have become the chief of a small tribe, all of which goes to show how strong is the call of the blood, and how deeply rooted in human nature is the longing for freedom and primitive independence, facts which, according to my own observations in Mexico, are not proven by single individuals only but by entire tribes as well.

The settlements herein described soon attracted a large number of families, some of them remaining in the little village of San Saba. The district was organized; a courthouse was built, likewise a schoolhouse capable of accommodating a larger number of pupils. Some small storekeepers began to do business, a saddler and blacksmith opened establishments, and the little town became the center of the surrounding districts which were just beginning to attract prospective settlers. San Saba was in possession of valuable waterpower resources produced by springs which gushed forth from the rocks near town. They had been used to operate a small corn mill which had now become inadequate to supply the demands of an

St. Jude Children's®
Research Hospital

Finding cures. Saving children.
ALSAC · DANNY THOMAS, FOUNDER

stjude.org/givehope

HOPE YOU ENJOY
this BOOK AS
MuCh AS I DID

Jerry

9-4-25

9A1

ever-increasing population. Besides, the settlers began to plant wheat in greater quantities, as the virgin soil seemed especially adapted to its cultivation and would produce as much as two hundred bushels to the acre, a record never surpassed in America either before or afterward, the average production throughout the United States being only about one-third of the record mentioned.

The small mill in San Saba belonged to Messrs. Brown and Williams, wealthy people who now invited me to devise a plan to increase the waterpower so as to enable them to add not only a sawmill, but also a good-sized flour mill to their plant. As people with technical knowledge and ability could not be found in the community, they delegated to me the task of constructing and installing the plant. *We moved there at once, and I built a small two-room frame house, which was the twelfth building put up in the town, and for us, the first self-owned home. Emily became very ill; wasting away, and my old friend Dr. Rogan insisted that she change climate for a while. I could not leave my new venture, so Emily undertook the long trip by stage to Meyersville, where she remained for a few months with her sister, Minna (Mrs. Mike Schiwetz).*

To my regret I found that the waterpower was insufficient to operate both mills at the same time, so the sawmill had to be operated by day and the flour mill by night. In the construction and management of corn mills and sawmills I was fairly well informed, but I had no experience whatever in operating a flour mill, and much was to be learned in this respect, as it was not profitable to leave too much of the flour in the hulls or to pulverize them; on the contrary, they had to be kept as intact as possible. Then, too, the summer wheat demanded a different treatment than the winter wheat, and there were many other such considerations. The flour mill had larger millstones and these were harder to sharpen, requiring more exact work since the rills and panels were flat instead of deep as in corn mills, and I experienced peculiar difficulties in keeping the panels straight and level, but by the aid of my keen eyesight, much patience and effort, I accomplished my task. This small plant had to provide all the population within a radius of fifty miles with flour and lumber, or until new settlements and communities became strong enough to support their own mills. The people of the newly organized counties of Eastland, Comanche, and Brown had the greatest difficulty in reaching us on account of distance, and when they came they brought great oxcarts loaded with the wheat of different families to be exchanged for flour. Sometimes these caravans had to wait a whole week before their turn came. The farmers nearby brought their wheat in on horseback and there were frequent quarrels between those who insisted on their flour being given them instantly and those who had to wait their regular turn. Some of the latter employed their spare time by getting beastly drunk and raising quarrels which were settled, as usual, with the six-shooter. These were not the types of the Tennessee and Kentucky settlers with whom I enjoyed the most friendly relations, but rather the Helena type of folks who had come from places of similar reputation and character. One of them by the name of Crosby had threatened several times to shoot me if his sack was not ready by noon.[2] One morning he came to the mill in a drunken condition and repeated the threat. As several people had arrived before he put in his appearance, I could not comply with his wish and really expected him to make good his threat. When he entered the door of the mill at noon he aimed his rifle at me and amidst curses and imprecations cocked both hammers. I jumped aside and, quickly seizing my heavy Colt's revolver, knocked the barrel of his rifle upward, which was discharged and tore a hole in the roof. I then knocked him down with the butt-end of my gun. There was one eyewitness to this encounter, a man by the name of Garbrough, who helped me in the mill work for several weeks. Of course I was arrested but after a few hours released on bond.

At the trial there were two contradictory statements by witnesses. Garbrough tried to prove that I had been the aggressor, while Mrs. Ward, the wife of the merchant, told the jury that from her open window she had heard Crosby boast to his brother-in-law that he had come to town to blow my brains out. This decided the case in my favor. I was acquitted, and a few years later was glad to learn that Crosby had completely recovered.

A month later Emily returned in good health to San Saba, but the days of our stay there were numbered. On account of the heavy wheat crop, I had to remain during nights at the mill to supervise

[2] In his "Some Notes for My Children," pp. 10–11, Krueger identifies his antagonist at San Saba as Hudspeth.

the grinding. Some intimate friends of Crosby's now tried to get even with me by shooting into the mill whenever we were grinding wheat. *Poor Emily insisted on staying at nights with me at the mill and she became very nervous, to the extent that we made up our minds to move back to civilization, that is, to Fredericksburg.*

I now sorely needed relaxation because the hard work at the circular saw and the night watches at the flour mill had exhausted my strength. Quiet little Fredericksburg seemed to be the best resting place.

This city was inhabited mainly by Germans. With all their good qualities, they are very clannish, and a newcomer was not welcomed. I had taken a job to run the Basse steam sawmill and liked my work, but jealousy of the old gang made it impossible for me to remain.

We had rented the little Langerhaus place, consisting of one room and kitchen, had bought a little more furniture and just begun to live in some comfort, and did not want to leave again. Since I could not find any work in the town, I bought a small farm for eight hundred dollars. My first payment was two hundred dollars, leaving two hundred dollars as a nest egg of the four hundred dollars that we had saved in San Saba.

The corn crop had already been gathered, but the fine grass growing was ripe for mowing. Near San Saba it was unnecessary to make hay, as grass for grazing purposes was plentiful, and being inexperienced in the art of making hay and impatient besides, I gathered it too soon and too green. Placed in my primitive barn, it caught fire by spontaneous combustion. I lost not only my hay but my barn as well, after I had been its owner for a little more than a month.

For a few weeks I tried to make a living by constructing saddletrees, but being too impatient even for this kind of work, I established myself as a sign painter and succeeded. The little town had never sheltered an artist of similar pretensions, so I had plenty of work, until finally every business house was decorated with a sign and both work and earnings stopped at the same time. Just at this stage of my career I inherited a sum of money in Germany, but I had to return to that country to collect it personally.

Letters came from my mother and Uncle Staewen urging me

to return. Staewen at that time was a large stockholder of the Vulcan at Stettin and offered to give me a good position where I could make a living easier than what I had been able to do here. Emily and I agreed that I should investigate this offer, and we supposed that I could return inside of four months. The nest egg of two hundred dollars was equally divided, and Emily remained in Fredericksburg while I started my journey to Germany with five twenty-dollar goldpieces.

Back to the Fatherland

MY first return to the land of my fathers was beset with many difficulties. As far as the city of Austin I used the overland stagecoach, known in those days all over the West and as far as California. These coaches were big, lumbering affairs, and they had to traverse rough stretches of country at a gallop wherever possible, and great care had to be taken lest the coaches fall to pieces. They had no springs to reduce the severe shocks produced by rough roads, and in their place the body was suspended by long, wide, and very strong leather straps. In this way the lateral motion of the coach was somewhat mitigated, but the shocks produced by its longitudinal motion were almost beyond endurance. It resembled the rolling of a vessel at sea when its bow and stern are alternately tossed by the waves. Feeble travelers usually became seasick during a long journey. The four spirited horses were exchanged at stations fifteen to twenty miles apart. The drivers were heavily armed, as the travelers were frequently waylaid by robbers. The passengers too were usually armed, for the country was still infested by marauding Indians.

From Austin to Galveston I rode on the train, having decided to sail from that port. At that time few people took passage to Europe from Galveston, so when I was informed that the small English steamer *San Jacinto* was ready to sail for Liverpool in three weeks, I decided to cross the ocean in that vessel. My finances being limited, I accepted a position with the Galveston Street Car Company in order to save some money. Electric street cars had not come into use at that time. Each car was drawn by two mules which were not hitched side by side but in single file, one behind the other. When a new supply of these animals was needed, the wild and unbroken mules of West Texas were purchased. As I was experienced in handling or breaking mules, a herd of them was entrusted to my training. After a week's sojourn in Galveston I made the acquaintance of Arthur and Ernest Wimer, two young Germans who owned a small bank in the city. The elder brother was preparing to make a short trip and asked me to pass the night in his home and take care of it during his absence, thus enabling me to save the expense of lodgings. It was the time of the yellow fever epidemic in Galveston, and during the third night I was there I suffered an attack of this terrible disease. I was removed to the City Hospital but soon dismissed as cured, and I could congratulate myself for having escaped with my life, as the number of patients who died from the disease was unusually large.

I found the steamer *San Jacinto* still lying in the harbor for some urgent repairs which had delayed its scheduled departure. I had become emaciated by the attack of yellow fever and my strength returned slowly. My cash had nearly dwindled away on account of hospital and medical expenses, but as I had determined not to postpone my journey any longer, I engaged to work as a stoker for my passage. The captain of the *San Jacinto* was a rough and unsociable Englishman. Never during all my passage did I hear him utter one kind word to any member of his crew. Strong as a bull and given to drinking, he uttered nothing but oaths and blasphemies and mistreated the poor cabin-boys with kicks and beatings. Our breakfast usually consisted of a flour or potato soup and hardtack, and our dinner was always the same—potatoes and salt pork. Our supper was made up of tea, herring, biscuit, and a glass of rum. As I did not like rum, I gladly shared my ration with other members of the crew, thereby winning their good will, for I was the only German on board. But the work on the steamer surpassed my strength because there was no arrangement whatever for ventilating the hot boiler room and the fine coal dust almost took my breath away. After two hours of working I fainted, and since the efforts of my mates did not revive me, they dragged me into a cabin and left me there without any assistance until the next day. Steamers of the *San Jacinto* type did not have doctors or surgeons, nor did they depend on steam power alone for their passage, using their sails for days at a stretch when the wind was favorable and thus saving much coal.

Upon my request to be allowed to work in the open air until I had regained my strength, I was allotted to one of the four-hour watches of the crew. We suffered from cold winds accompanied by much rain, but I was more inconvenienced than my fellow-sailors on account of my clothing. At four o'clock in the morning the deck had to be washed. While doing this work the other sailors wore trousers and oilskin jackets and long heavy leather boots. My clothes consisted of the light cotton fabric generally worn in Texas. Naturally I got soaking wet every morning after a short time spent at deck-washing; besides, I had to stand the four-hour watch in wet clothing and in a raging wind. But more difficult was the night work, when we had to climb the tall masts in dark and rainy weather and, clinging to the highest yards, had to reef the sails. As a boy I had been a good "turner," well trained in gymnastics, and during my long stay in the wilderness I had grown supple and entirely fearless, but in spite of all this I often felt that I could not trust my weight to my arms.

Five days after our departure from Galveston we doubled the south coast of Florida and were surprised by a sudden calm and a rapid fall of the mercury. Within an hour it became as dark as if night had settled on us, although it was still afternoon. Shortly afterward the wind came in heavy gusts, causing the ship to tremble from deck to keel, and then the rage of the storm broke forth, increasing from minute to minute. All sails were reefed in and every movable object on deck secured with double ropes. The mate informed me we had passed into one of those ever-recurring West Indian hurricanes, and that we would have a bad night of it. The storm now lashed the waves to enormous heights. We closed all the skylights and all sailors remaining on deck had to secure themselves with ropes to prevent being washed overboard. The first damage we incurred was the loss of a small part of the officer's bridge. At midnight the shift to which I belonged was on duty. We lashed ourselves to a rope, for every wave striking the vessel broadside caused it to flounder and tilt so much that its yards touched the waters of the sea. One wave after another came rolling on, tearing at the cable that held us fast. The fury of the hurricane increased more and more, and the howling and roaring of the wind became so loud that one could not understand what his nearest companion was shouting. The number of officers on the bridge was doubled. The screw was in the water part of the time and part of the time in the air, when it would revolve with mad rapidity. Suddenly a sail was torn loose, bringing down the top mast. Both watches were called on deck to begin the dangerous task of cutting the ropes clear from the broken mast. But our efforts were in vain, for the fallen mast, dangling overboard on its cordage, became entangled in the screw; both of the blades and the rudder were broken, and we drifted helplessly in the turmoil of the seething water. Without screw and rudder it was impossible to steer the ship against the waves. Every man thought his last hour was at hand and all hope of rescue was abandoned, and as we were exhausted by overexertion, we became indifferent to the doom which the next few minutes seemed to hold in store for us. From hour to hour double rations of rum were served and every sailor looked around for a place of safety. But with the falling of the mast the fury of the storm seemed to abate itself somewhat, apparently content with the havoc it had wrought. Our spirits rose again. However, it was not until noon the next day that the waters became less turbulent. Meanwhile, the deck was cleared of all wreckage.

We now drifted into the Gulf Stream in which we slowly passed into calmer waters and were carried along toward the Florida coast not more than ten miles distant. Toward midnight we sighted the lights of a giant steamer, which, attracted by our signal flares, promised to lay by till morning and take us in tow. This steamer was bound for Norfolk, Virginia, and several days later we landed in this port. I remained a few days longer on the *San Jacinto*, but when I was told that the repairs would require at least a month's time I engaged passage on another English steamer. Two weeks later I landed at Liverpool and arrived at Berlin the following week without further mishaps.

Upon my arrival, a family meeting was held to decide on my future. The verdict came quick enough. Uncle Staewen would give me a good position at the Vulcan, on the condition that I would not return to America and would abandon and separate from my wife,

*because they did not believe that a Texas woman would be their
equal socially. Having left Emily behind with eye trouble, which
made it difficult for her to write me, I became most anxious to return
home quickly but had no means to carry out this plan. My grand-
father Bremer had set aside for me five hundred dollars which I was
to receive when I became of age; this money I now collected and,
knowing that photographic galleries were very scarce in Texas, I
learned photography in a Berlin gallery.*

The art of photography, which came into use in Germany some
twenty years before my return to that country, had made great
strides, and I was struck by the thought of introducing this art in
Texas, where only small tintypes, called "ferrotypes," were made. I
served an apprenticeship of six weeks in a well-known photo-studio,
after which I invested my entire inheritance in a complete photographic outfit. For portraits I purchased a Bush lens, for landscapes
a Steinheil aplanatic lens, and tickets, album paper, glass plates for
negatives, and all the necessary chemicals. Everything was carefully
packed and shipped to my home in the New World. At first I had
great difficulties on account of the tropical heat, as it was impossible
to get ice to cool the chemical preparations. The silver bath crys-
tallized, causing the collodion film covering the glass plates to be
dotted with little holes. The oxide of iron and pyrogallic acids easily spoiled. The sensitive emulsion paper dried too fast after being
treated in the silver bath and turned yellow. These and many other
similar difficulties I had to overcome by patient and constant inves-
tigation and experiments. As one little town alone could not furnish
sufficient patronage, I constructed a tent about thirty feet long and
visited all the settlements from the Texas coast to San Saba. I remained at a place about a week and not only earned sufficient money
for my needs but had an opportunity to get acquainted with a great
many people of that period. *I made some money, but life was not a
pleasant one, being away from home most of the time. Our oldest
son, Willy, was born during this time (May 2, 1874).*

After two years of wandering I sold my entire outfit to Mr. Fey,
a young man whose descendants still conduct the studio at Cuero,
Texas, or did at the time this was written. In addition to making
portraits I was fond of photographing landscapes, and to this very

day I have religiously preserved pictures made fifty years ago because the majority of the people I photographed have long since
passed away.[1]

[1] Unfortunately, Krueger's collection of photographs has been lost. A determined search by his family has yielded only one picture, that of a servant
at a hotel in Boerne. As Krueger was one of the first photographers in Texas
and this single example of his work is of interesting composition, the loss of
his collection is indeed regrettable.

A Manhunt

FURTHER back I said that we wanted to get back to civilization and moved to Fredericksburg. The kind of civilization that existed there, the following incident will show.

It was the time of the cattlemen's war in the frontier counties. The leaders of the opposing parties were Lemberg and Bader of Llano County and Gladden and Beard of Mason County.[1]

Midway between San Saba and Fredericksburg I came to the banks of the beautiful Llano River and spent the night at the home of the then noted cattle king Lemberg. His wife told me that he had been moving a great herd of cattle to Kansas and had just recently returned. His neighbors had entrusted Lemberg with a part of their livestock and Lemberg had agreed to reimburse them from the proceeds on his return, but the market had been unfavorable, the expense greater than anticipated, and Lemberg was compelled to accept low prices and return without the necessary means to take care of his obligations. A party of Americans of the Helena type, led by Moses Beard and Tom Gladden, were not satisfied with Lemberg's explanation and had made several attempts on his life. Even during

[1] Krueger was involved in one of the last episodes of the Mason County, or Hoodoo, War. See Stella Gipson Polk, *Mason and Mason County: A History* (Austin: Pemberton Press, 1966), pp. 48–59; and C. L. Sonnichsen, *Ten Texas Feuds* (Albuquerque: University of New Mexico Press, 1971), pp. 87–107. Sonnichsen identifies the leaders of the war as George Gladden and brothers Mose and John Beard on one side and brothers Charley and Peter Bader on the other. Both Mose Beard and Charley Bader had been killed by the time Krueger entered the scene. Interestingly, Krueger sees no overtones of racial conflict between German and Anglo settlers as do some writers.

the night which I passed in his home many shots were fired into the house and his wife and children were forced to hide in the cellar. I then discovered that Lemberg himself was hiding in the house, and during the quiet hours of dawn he told me the history of his misfortunes and entreated me to try to negotiate with his enemies, as all his efforts to find a suitable man for this delicate task had failed. The complaining parties lived at Loyal Valley, a distance of twenty miles from the Llano River, and after a few days I succeeded in effecting a compromise settlement, a bank at Austin agreeing to guarantee the amount to be reimbursed by Lemberg.

Mr. Bader, a German, had had similar difficulties with the Loyal Valley people, who would not listen to reason or argument. *To protect his family, he had brought them down to Fredericksburg. He had made arrangements to move to Florida but had to visit Lemberg in Llano for a final settlement, and his enemies, knowing this, were laying for him. During my short stay at Fredericksburg I became acquainted with Bader, and at different times he begged me to make the trip with him. Just to tease him I held out with my right hand an old watch, saying, if you can hit the center of the watch, I shall go with you. Like lightning he turned his horse, pulled his Winchester, and shot the dead center out of my watch. So I had to join him on this dangerous ride.*

We left Fredericksburg at noon intending to spend the first night at the home of another German, Baron Marschall von Bieberstein. He was the son of a German minister in one of the small Hessian principalities, if I am not mistaken, and had joined the "Mainzer Adels-Verein" for emigration and was raising sheep near the so-called House Mountain. When we had traveled about halfway, we met five men on horseback headed by Beard and Gladden. Recognition of us on their part meant immediate trouble. Bader and I sought cover among the thick bushes, but our pursuers were well mounted and now began a regular manhunt which was long remembered by the cattlemen of the neighborhood. Bader and I had fast horses and excellent rifles, and both of us were good marksmen. Bader had been reared in these mountains and knew every nook and crook in them. We were about 250 yards ahead of Beard and Gladden and tried to increase the distance as much as possible. The many bullets whizzing around us did no more damage than to shatter Bader's saddle horn, but it was a very disagreeable kind of music to our ears. Finally we started firing back at our pursuers, but as our horses were going at a fast clip, our shots went wild.

We had to cover seven miles before we reached von Marschall's house, and although we had to rest our horses from time to time, we still gained on our enemies and reached our destination safely after all. In order not to endanger von Marschall's family by the firing of Beard and Gladden's gang, we entrenched ourselves for the night in a log cabin used for a stable and far enough from the residence to ensure safety to the occupants. We barricaded the place as well as we could, and when darkness came on we could see the campfires from Beard and Gladden's camp. All we could do was to await the dawn of day if our lives were to be spared. Bader resolved to remain several days with von Bieberstein, while I succeeded in stealing past our adversaries and reached Fredericksburg about noon sound and well.

Poor Bader fared worse. Fear for the safety of his family made him leave his shelter sooner than he had intended. Toward ten o'clock in the morning, when Beard and his party had withdrawn for a while, Bader tried to break through their lines and reach Lemberg's home, but his enemies lay in ambush for him and he was killed four miles from von Bieberstein's home. His body was cut into pieces and ruthlessly suspended from the branches of a nearby liveoak tree.[2]

Only one more trip did I make with my photographic outfit, and this was to the Lemberg store on the Llano. With much danger to my own life, I was able to adjust matters between the warring parties, and the State Rangers who came to Lemberg after the Bader killing could return to Austin, as the guerrilla war was ended.

[2] Peter Bader was killed January 20, 1876, and George Gladden was sent to prison for the murder (Sonnichsen, *Ten Texas Feuds*, p. 107).

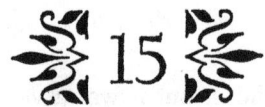

At Twin Sisters

DURING my wanderings as an itinerant photographer I saw a place in Blanco County which had a special charm for me. Located in a valley five miles from two hills called the Twin Sisters, it was a very productive and beautiful region. The country was bounded on the south by the Guadalupe River and watered by the two Blanco rivers, while the northern part was traversed by Miller Creek and the Pedernales River. I now had some means of my own and would have liked to return to my old love of stock-raising, but the times had changed. The government did not make any more land grants. Land had to be bought, although the price was exceedingly low. The raising of livestock necessitated extensive pastures, at least ten thousand acres, and I could not afford such a sum at this time. A strong wave of immigrants from the northern states had flooded many sections, and large tracts of land had been granted to the railroads, or rather to their promoters. Within ten years—from 1870 to 1880—this immense territory had been covered with a network of railroads, all of which were built in return for land grants. State subsidies had also been granted, and it was obvious that in the thinly settled parts of the country the railroads would not prove to be profitable for many years to come.

So I established with my limited means a country store in the neighborhood of Twin Sisters. Such a store had to carry in stock all kinds of fabrics, ready-made garments, shoes, hats, ironware, provisions, and many other things, as the customers living at a great distance from the store could not afford to frequent it more than once a week and sometimes once a month and preferred to make large and more profitable purchases. Cash money was scarce, and frequently I had to take in its place horses, cattle, rawhides, and sometimes parts of the crops. Especially in corn I carried on an extensive trade, as I could sell this product or a large part of it to the various military stations, and again, as in San Saba, I built a steam-driven corn mill.

With the exception of Willy and Marguerite, all of our children were born in the dwelling connected with the store, and for nearly twenty-five years we made it our home in joy and sorrow, failure and success. I did my own freighting, and while I was on the road, Emily had to wait on customers, who were mostly German farmers, thrifty and honest. The business grew and soon I could afford to keep a clerk.

Right here I should like to say a few words about the pioneer women and their work. Most of them were excellent housekeepers and cooks, grew their own vegetables, and helped the menfolk in the fields, but they lacked education, showing little interest in flowers and fancy work. They were experienced and indefatigable workers at the spinning wheel and hand loom but unskilled in making any except the simplest and coarsest kinds of clothing. Among these people, then, was the proper place for my wife to be of service to the community and make the best use of her accomplishments. She came from a fine German family which had settled in Texas in the fifties; she had acquired an excellent education and was skilled in all kinds of fancy work. She instructed the young girls gratis in tailoring, crochet work, and embroidering, and soon a marked improvement and progress could be perceived in the general appearance of the women, and their sphere of life. The young ladies boasted of better-fitting dresses, handmade laces, and little flower gardens in front of their homes. Heretofore, the only head-dress worn by the women was the familiar sunbonnet made of plain cotton material to protect the face from the dazzling sun. Now they were adorned with embroidery of choice material and harmonious colors which plainly proved their growing interest in finer and more elegant articles of apparel.

Appreciating my wife's wholesome influence, these simple people did everything in their power to reciprocate her services. In spite of this work my wife found time to tend her flower garden and raise fine vegetables which she sold to travelers and in this way added many dollars to our savings.

I was extremely busy, as I had been appointed postmaster in addition to my many other duties, and a year later I was elected justice of the peace. Civil cases not involving large sums came under my jurisdiction, and cases of assault, which were very frequent, also had to be tried in my court. I studied the laws diligently in order to give intelligent instructions to the jury, and a number of young lawyers practiced in my court who later became celebrated members of the Texas bar. Three of them particularly I recall—Judge Bill Martin, Judge Storey, and Tom Ward. While serving as justice of the peace it was my duty to officiate at weddings, but this did not require a long time. The simple marriage ceremony was read from the statutes, and when the all important "Yes" had been pronounced, it was certified by witnesses. The marriage fee was five dollars, and gladly have I made many couples happy for that price. But I was disappointed on a certain occasion when William Haas, an acquaintance of mine, whose children and grandchildren now live in Blanco County, came to me one day with his bride to be married. Both were of German descent, and I tried to make the ceremony particularly solemn and impressive, and for the occasion I composed a nice address in German teeming with eloquent passages from German authors. I quoted Schiller's beautiful lines: "Honor to woman! To her it is given to garland the earth with the roses of heaven." I committed it to memory and it made a deep impression on the couple, the bride being moved to tears, as she had never before heard anything so beautiful. Naturally I expected an extra fee for this effort, but after the ceremony Haas came to me and said rather bashfully that as everything had been so solemn and beautiful, he would not insult me by offering me the customary five-dollar fee, but that he and his wife would reward me with their undying gratitude instead. Needless to remark that after this experience I conscientiously adhered to the simple marriage ceremony provided for in the statutes.

Now I began to feel rather proud of my success and my achievements, and it was my intention to attempt to transplant German cordiality and sociability in this foreign land. To this end I built a dance pavilion and bowling alley. It was difficult to furnish dance music, as regular musicians were unknown quantities at that time. But I purchased a large German organ which was used by the young people. The beer necessary for such occasions was imported from St. Louis but came to be too expensive on account of the transportation charges. Suddenly a bright idea struck me. Knowing that beer contained water as its principal base, I added to my other ventures a small brewery, in which business, however, I did not prosper. My knowledge of the art of brewing was derived from a booklet entitled "How to Make Beer." The difficulty was that I did not make the beer for myself but for other people; consequently, it had to be good. Several experiments on a minor scale failed on account of the high temperature, which was not surprising, as we did not have either natural or artificial ice for cooling the product; it therefore turned to vinegar and my speculation came to naught. And I did not fare any better with the dance hall. A great many young pistol-toters and bullies flocked to the place from the more distant settlements, and after they had imbibed copious drams of bad whiskey which they had brought with them, the usual brawls and fights started. Several persons were badly wounded, but I did not care to employ my medical skill acquired at San Saba; furthermore, I did not deem it compatible with the dignity of a judge and postmaster to operate a dance hall, so the place was discontinued and converted into a warehouse.

To humor an old Methodist friend at San Saba, I constructed a small cotton gin for cleaning cotton fibres from the seed. I wished to encourage this old fellow to plant cotton, and this first experiment succeeded better than we anticipated. This was the first experiment in raising cotton in such a high altitude, and today cotton growing is the most profitable branch of agriculture in the entire community.

At Twin Sisters in Blanco County, where I now resided, more cotton was planted the following year, but to have it ginned the farmers had to haul the raw cotton a great distance. So the idea to build a modern cotton gin did not require much deliberation; therefore, I purchased a complete steam-driven outfit from my old friend Walter Tips at Austin.

Cottonseed, which is about the size of the Mexican bean and contains a kernel rich in oil, is generally planted toward the end of

March to about the middle of April. It is planted in rows about three feet apart. After the young plants have sprouted they are thinned out in such a manner that the distance from one plant to another is about two feet. If cool nights prevail, the young plants will die and have to be replanted. The freezing point is thirty-two degrees Fahrenheit, but young cotton plants will die even at thirty-eight degrees. About two months after planting the cotton stalks attain a height of about two feet and produce their first blossoms. They continue to bloom as long as weather conditions are favorable. A large cottonfield presents a beautiful sight. In the morning the blossoms are pink and yellow, but pale during the day to a yellowish white. On a single stalk there may sometimes be counted as many as fifty blossoms. The boll next develops very rapidly and when full grown is about the size of a small chicken egg. Within two months after the first bloom appears the bolls burst open and the snow-white cotton matures. The field now appears dotted with snowballs dangling from the bolls, between which fresh blossoms continue to appear. Not every blossom develops into a boll, however, because many are cast off and fall to the ground, but with a growth of about twenty bolls to the stalk, a fertile soil will produce a bale of cotton to the acre. A bale is equal to five hundred pounds of lint cotton, or about sixteen hundred pounds of raw cotton still containing the seed. The cotton gin is made to clean the cotton from its seed and to compress it by high steam power into a marketable bale. The average per acre as indicated should be the rule, but the cotton plant is subject to so many parasites and enemies that a quarter of a bale to the acre may be said to be an average crop. One of the greatest pests is the webworm, which spins its web around the young plant during wet periods and strangles it. Another pestiferous parasite is the army worm, which destroys the leaves of entire cottonfields within a few days. But the most pernicious pest is the boll weevil. A little buglike parasite hardly any larger than a grain of wheat is the boll weevil. This insect taps the young boll and deposits its eggs in it. These develop into worms, and when they begin to grow the boll drops from the stalk and the tiny creatures change into a chrysalis and give life to scores of young weevils. To protect the cotton plant from this pest, the farmer very often has to resort to sprinkling his cotton stalks with poisonous liquids, especially arsenic solutions, but sometimes even these remedies avail nothing.

Cotton gathering or picking cotton usually starts about the first of August. Men, women, and children pick the dry cotton, which contains the seed. With nimble fingers it is gathered and placed in sacks, and as they are filled, the sacks are taken to a wagon kept in waiting in the field, to be weighed and emptied. An average cotton picker is able to pick two hundred pounds a day, while an extra-good picker can gather from three to four hundred pounds a day. Negroes and Mexicans are the most expert pickers. When approximately sixteen hundred pounds of raw cotton have been deposited in the wagon, it is hauled to the nearest gin to be ginned.

The entire arrangement of a modern cotton gin is worked pneumatically. The loaded wagon is placed under a pipe which is joined to a vacuum fan, which sucks the cotton into the cleaners where it is separated from leaves, dirt, and other foreign substances. By its own weight and by means of an ingenious contrivance the cotton now drops into the gin stand proper, which consists of a revolving cylinder of circular saws about three-fourths of an inch apart, between which iron ribs are fastened one-fourth of an inch apart and above the saws. Through their interstices the cotton is drawn by the fine teeth of the saws, and after being forced by cylindrical brushes into a sheet-iron pipe several feet in diameter to the condenser, thence to the hydraulic press, while the seed is conveyed into the seed house and kept there until it is taken to an oil mill for crushing and refining.

As I have mentioned elsewhere, raw cotton consists of two-thirds of seed and one-third of lint or pure cotton fibre. Fifty years ago there was no known way of utilizing this seed, one-half of which contains a very palatable oil, while the other half is composed of a very nutritious meal which is now extensively used for feeding cattle. During slavery times the Negroes on some of the plantations were fed on cottonseed, but in some instances death resulted, and as a slave at that time was worth approximately $1,500, Indian corn was substituted.

I can remember the time when cottonseed was used only as a fertilizer, then only in small quantities for gardens. Great heaps were piled up near every cotton gin, and we frequently paid fifty cents a load to have them hauled away. At present the oil mills pay more than a dollar a hundred pounds for cottonseed, and they have become a source of great profit to the cotton farmer.

In the cottonseed oil mills the last fibres are separated from the seed, and the hulls are removed by a machine until nothing remains but the pure kernel. The hulls are used to feed cattle, while the kernels after being heated in retorts are conducted into hydraulic presses where the last remnants of oil are extracted, and nothing remains but the flat cottonseed meal cakes, which are exported to all parts of the world. For feeding purposes, these cakes are ground and together with the hulls make an ideal food for cattle.

The crude cottonseed oil obtained by the process described is dark in color and must be refined. By the use of small gauged sieves the greater part of the refuse is removed, but the fine yellow transparency is imparted to the oil by heating and adding a certain quantity of light-colored Texas clay. By constant stirring with this clay the last impurities are eliminated and the oil is ready for use. Mixed with tallow it makes the well-known margarine. It is also used in mixing dyes for industrial purposes. It is fully equal to olive oil in color and quality, and shiploads of it are sent to France and Italy and returned to us neatly bottled and labeled as genuine olive oil.

The average cotton crop in Texas at present is nearly four million bales of five hundred pounds each. At a price of twenty cents a pound, the revenue from a single crop amounts to four hundred million dollars. To this must be added the value of the seed, worth approximately twenty to thirty dollars a ton, and the oil and cottonseed meal, hulls, and cake, which brings this total to a much greater sum.

The whole settlement united in many sport gatherings that the Germans like so well. Carl Wenzel organized a singing society, which joined the Mountain Sangerbund, and many festivities were the result in nearby cities. This ideal life was suddenly broken up by a political body named the Party of the Middle of the Road. Their teachings were that no middleman was needed between consumer and producer. New union stores belonging to Farmers' Union were established, and old friendships turned into jealousy and hatred. Our business also felt the effect, and I carried out my old plan to go into the ranch business on a larger scale.

Every year while operating my store at Twin Sisters, I had to take a number of young steers in exchange for merchandise. I sold them very profitably to big ranchers who did not raise their own cattle. They in turn profited by buying young animals which they fattened on cheap pastures and shipped to northern markets or sold to big companies which limited their activities to fattening cattle. The high prices I received when I had accumulated a large number of yearlings enabled me to realize a profit on my merchandise. In addition to a few hundred head of steers left me by my customers in exchange for goods, I bought during the next few years about a thousand or fifteen hundred young steers from distant settlements. Every spring for a number of years I stocked the great Las Moras Ranch in this way. This ranch was 150 miles distant in Menard County and was owned by the Runge family of Galveston. The elder brother, Julius Runge, a prosperous merchant of considerable means, was the German consul for many years, but unfortunately lost his wealth in cotton speculation, and his fine estate passed into other hands.

In order to be able to provide for so great a number of cattle as I was constantly acquiring, I purchased the Twin Sisters and the old Evans ranches, together with the adjoining properties, and soon had a pasture of ten thousand acres. For ranching purposes I needed these properties, and to reap the full benefits of them I took up cattle raising as a permanent business.

Just at this time barbed wire was invented and came into general use, causing great changes in agriculture and stock raising. As the beautiful valleys could be fenced at small cost and the crops protected from the depredations of wild cattle, agriculture advanced at a rapid rate. Still greater was the influence exerted by the use of barbed wire on the breeding of livestock, as in pastures thus fenced everybody was able to have his cattle under daily control and surveillance.

My first investment was the purchase of one thousand purebred sheep, and I engaged a Mexican to look after them. These sheep were housed in their pens every night and proved to be a profitable speculation, as I obtained from them about six thousand pounds of the best wool, for which I received twenty cents a pound. The sale of the fattened mutton further increased my revenue, and the natural propagation of lambs always tallied with the diminution of the herd through sales. The length of my wire fence was nearly thirty miles and it required almost a year to finish it. I was now getting in a position to indulge in cattle raising, my favorite occupation, to my heart's content. The proprietors, being able to have their herds under continual supervision, now turned their attention to improving their stock. The best and most valuable bulls of the Hereford and Durham breeds were imported from the northern states and from England. Even from India the Zebus or sacred bulls of Brahma were purchased at great cost and crossed with Texas cattle. At the livestock expositions at Chicago and in England I had seen the Red Poll breeds which particularly appealed to my fancy. Their color was dark red, only the tips of their tails being white. Born without horns, they had no desire to gore one another and remained peaceful and gentle during the time of their feeding. By crossing them with native cattle I succeeded in breeding large, sound, and healthy animals possessing all the qualities of the imported bulls. The halfbreeds in particular remained without horns and displayed the same fine darkred color. The dairy cattle were also greatly improved. For butter the trim little Jerseys were raised, but for milch-cows Holstein and Frisian breeds were imported. Since these new and better breeds had to be fed during the winter season, fodder was more extensively raised on most of the ranches. And now the cottonseed so long despised and without market value came into its own for its nourishing qualities.

In spite of all the hard work I passed many happy hours on the Twin Sisters Ranch. Objects of special pride were my saddle and carriage horses, and to this day I pity those city people who have never had the opportunity of possessing such a noble animal as the horse and being permitted to get acquainted with its character and peculiarities. To the city man a horse is a horse. He does not know how many qualities it has in common with man. Jealousy, for instance, is a trait which man shares with many quadrupeds. Usually, when a stallion is left with several mares for a few months to bring about some sort of family life, he will pay his first attentions to the finest creature in the herd. If he favors one of the mares with special consideration, the slighted ones will try to get revenge by biting and kicking her in the absence of the stallion. Man, too, usually prefers some certain one of his kind over all others and will treat her with extreme tenderness and consideration. In the case of animals, the favored one grows very devoted and ever tries to be near its benefactor.

I was often compelled to use my horses monstrously hard and long at times, and the almost human creatures knew very well how to impress me with this fact by stopping in the shade of a tree, turning their heads and beautiful eyes at me, and softly touching with their lips the leg used in dismounting. If I gave way to their appeals and took off the saddle, they gave a long groan of relief, and invariably rubbed their noses on the horny wart inside of their front legs. This seemed to give them new strength, and they would wallow in the dust to rid their bodies of the itching sweat. I cannot help thinking but that this wart on the inside of the horse's front legs is a source of secret energy, although I cannot prove it any more than our scientists can give a plausible explanation of the fact that a scorched finger instantly stops hurting when held to the flap of the ear. Nor can they explain why the heat of the sun is stronger at the inside of a window than at the outside. Still plainer is the language of the horse when the poor animal is to be remounted without being sufficiently rested. By all kinds of tricks it refuses to take the bit, tries to escape when about to be burdened with the heavy saddle, deliberately practices deep breathing while its master is tightening up the girth, and assumes all kinds of queer positions when he tries to leap in the saddle. I well remember one occasion when I was in high school; our professor of natural history explained to us that the eye of the horse is a kind of magnifying lens representing a human being as a giant, and for this reason the horse is subject to man. Later on, as a cowboy, when I was able to throw a horse by main strength, I smiled when I recalled this theory of the professor.

In a book on human vanity the author remarks rather frivolously, I think, that some people like to ride fine horses in order to parade themselves and incite the envy of their fellow man. But I can assure my readers that the presence or absence of lookers-on made little difference with me, and that I enjoyed riding a fine horse just as well when alone and no human being was in evidence to be made envious.

To improve my grazing lands, I imported and planted foreign

grass seed. After many years of experimenting I succeeded with the Bermuda grass. It was so prolific and vigorous that neither years of droughts nor excessive rains could prevent its roots from sprouting again and again. The other kinds of grass I experimented with prospered as long as they were well protected by careful cultivation but died when neglected and crowded out by the old indigenous grasses. A long time is required for some plants to be acclimated, even with suitable soil and climate, and I am of the opinion that the same altitudes and latitudes in the different parts of the world produce the same kinds of plants. My property in Texas was in the same latitude as Algiers in Africa, and when I later traveled in that country, I encountered to a certain extent the same flowers, grasses, and herbs I had known in Texas.

In the southern part of my Twin Sisters Ranch there was a cedar forest extending for several miles. It was practically impenetrable and especially hard to get through on horseback. It was in these forests that the most ferocious of my steers would remain in hiding. They simply could not be caught by ordinary means, so we trained two large shepherd dogs by using tame steers, one to seize the tail of the hunted animal and the other to grasp its muzzle. In the thick underbrush the steers could not move about fast enough to defend themselves, and after I had penetrated the forests several times on foot with my dogs I found downright pleasure in this dangerous sport. Our rear dog would sometimes be dragged several yards by hanging to the steer's tail, while the dog in front would hold to the steer's nose, refusing to let loose. Part of the time the front dog would be flying in the air and part of the time trailing on the ground, but he would never relinquish his muzzle-hold on the steer. Chased in this way, the steers were soon glad to seek the open prairie where some of our men would be waiting to corral them.

It was not, however, our friends and companions of the animal kingdom alone which kept alive my interest and always fascinated me, but also our enemies, especially the poisonous reptiles. I remember once having watched from morning till night to ascertain the time required for some animals to die from the bite of a rattlesnake. Hogs I found to be entirely immune, probably on account of their thick layers of fat which contain few blood vessels. On many occasions I could also observe how the bite of this reptile affects man.

The chemical analysis of rattlesnake poison shows albumen and formic acid to be the component parts. As both of these components, chemically mixed and injected into the veins of test-subjects, did not do any harm, there must still be other component parts which make rattlesnake poison so injurious. I also had opportunities to gather practical and firsthand experience in treating people bitten by rattlesnakes. The bite of this reptile is absolutely fatal within twenty-four hours if the poison enters a vein and is carried directly to the heart. Cutting out and cauterizing the wound is entirely useless in such cases, but if the poison is communicated to an artery, cutting and sucking the wound may do some good. Nevertheless the patient is generally attacked by violent and prolonged convulsions, and the principal source of relief and recovery are medicines instilled into the blood by way of the stomach. There is doubtless an acid in rattlesnake poison, and any substance capable of neutralizing an acid is worth trying, such as spirits of ammonia, sodium bicarbonate, or chalk. These should be applied to the wound and also taken internally in large doses, but even these remedies easily cause vomiting and are frequently ineffective. The surest remedy proved to be whiskey in excessive quantities. I have seen women and even children under such circumstances drink a whole quart of whiskey or other alcoholic liquids without becoming drunk, though under normal conditions a small quantity of liquor would have rendered them highly intoxicated.

I once trained a clever dog to chase rattlesnakes. His only protection against being bitten was in all probability his thick coat of long hair, but even without this protection a snake had little chance to bite him. Immediately on discovering a rattlesnake, he employed an old trick of jumping back when the snake coiled up and raised its head to strike at him, so that the fangs of the reptile could never touch his body. He would continue this line of attack for several minutes, sometimes for nearly an hour, or until the snake, becoming tired and unable to reach the dog, would try to escape. Then the dog would suddenly grasp the reptile's tail with his teeth and, after tossing it in the air several times, would seize it and crush its head.

Becoming interested in the breeding of hogs, I tried to diminish the cost of feeding, and after much hard work I finally succeeded in raising the "grunters" for the market at very little cost. We imported

Johnson grass from the Mississippi Valley and planted the seed in two acres of sandy loam, enclosing the acreage by a fence. The grass itself has no food value whatever, but it forms a network of succulent roots which soon cover the entire ground. These roots, which greatly resemble asparagus, are very nutritious, and after our field had been well covered with them, we turned fifty half-grown hogs into it. Every morning it was necessary to have a Negro plow up a few furrows to enable the hogs to get to the roots more easily, and in the fall of the year their weight would double. Unfortunately, the culture of Johnson grass had one great disadvantage; its seed was disseminated by the birds over wide areas, and when the grass had once obtained a firm growth in cultivated fields, it could not be exterminated, so in time the local officials forbade the further culture of this kind of grass.

Protected by numerous barbed wire fences, our cattle increased rapidly, as did the number of wolves, and the tracks of the latter could not be followed as easily as when the country was open and unfenced, which resulted in considerable damage being done to our sheep and calves. We used to hunt wolves with bloodhounds. One of my neighbors—a Mr. Heidrich—owned a pack of these valuable dogs, and Sunday afternoon was our favorite time for engaging in a wolf hunt, in which a half-dozen or more ranchmen would take part. Generally a pack of five or more wolves would be located by our dogs in the cedar forests, and the whole pack of bloodhounds turned loose and kept at their heels. After a chase of several miles the wolves would usually put up a fight and the older ones would have to be shot, while the younger ones usually escaped. During these wolf hunts many wire fences were cut and after the sport was all over these fences had to be repaired. This was always a tedious and disagreeable task.

The wire fences made it possible for the stockmen to raise nearly twice the number of cattle they had formerly raised, and by digging wells a sufficient supply of water could be provided, thus eliminating one of the serious handicaps of ranching, as water is as important to the cattle as food. Before the pastures could be fenced and drinking water provided, the cattle used to gather near a river or stream and would remain there feeding on such grass as they found near the water.

With the increase in the number of cattle, the demand decreased and the prices sank proportionately. To overcome a bad situation, we tried to promote the increase in steers and reduce the birth rate of cows. In the course of time conditions changed entirely. The price of cattle rose in the northern states and our entire stock of steers went to market to supply the demand which so diminished our herds that the price for cows increased and we received better prices for them than for steers. For some time stock-raising flourished and grazing lands advanced in price. Railroad mileage rapidly increased and breeders were able to ship their cattle in railroad cars. Furthermore, stock-raising was well protected by the tariff laws, and even the sheep raisers came in for a share of the prosperity, receiving as much as thirty cents a pound for their wool. These prosperous times were followed by an overproduction which caused a sharp slump in the price of cattle, and toward the end of the eighties cows could be bought in Texas for six to eight dollars a head. As the cost of raising cattle exceeded the selling price, the breeders rapidly became impoverished, especially those who had bought their pasture lands at high prices and were taxed proportionately higher. Many of the banks which financed the cattlemen demanded their loans, thus necessitating the sale of large herds at ruinous prices.

At the beginning of the nineties Grover Cleveland was elected president by the Democrats, and as soon as the party was in power the tariff on wool, hides, cattle, and sheep was removed.

Australia had accumulated great quantities of wool and soon flooded this country with the surplus product. I had hoped to get twenty-five cents for my wool but sold it in Boston for six cents a pound. Land which had been valued at reasonable prices during the preceding years could now be bought at ridiculously low figures and to all intents and purposes was worthless. Many of the small country banks became insolvent. Cash money was extremely scarce and longterm credits were no longer obtainable. Truly these were hard times, and many an excellent ranchman who had acquired wealth and prominence went bankrupt. But this was only the beginning of the crisis: the sequel was even worse.

Drought and Its Consequences

CONDITIONS now prevailed, the causes of which were hard to fathom. In the northern hemisphere the regions around the thirtieth parallel are most exposed to droughts, which seem to follow this line around the globe. In western America this belt extends from the thirty-fifth parallel to the twenty-fifth and comprises Mexico, Arizona and New Mexico, and the western part of Texas. In northern Africa this belt reaches even farther south, so that beginning with the thirtieth parallel the great desert of Sahara, the Libyan desert, Egypt, Arabia, and Persia all suffer from recurring droughts. My property was lying exactly on the thirtieth parallel of the northern latitude in Texas, and here especially in my daily struggles with the forces of nature I have made observations, which with my travels in Mexico, Arizona, and New Mexico, enabled me to make comparisons of conditions in those states with the conditions at home.

Now it should not be assumed that during these dry periods the clouds were always serene. The formation of clouds consequent to the evaporation of great masses of water on the globe remains practically the same, and regular wind currents generally carry those humid clouds over the same area. Thus rainclouds are formed over the Gulf of Mexico, destined to provide Texas with the necessary moisture, and are carried by southeast winds in a northwest direction over Texas, and the northern part of Mexico, Arizona, and New Mexico. But as the heat of the southern sun causes the north winds to assume the same high temperature, the clouds simply melt away when both these air currents meet, instead of condensing and precipitating in the form of much-needed rain. Although rain is caused by the meeting of a cold air current with a warm one, these cool northern currents are not the sole producers of rain, as violent thunderstorms are likely to occur during the hottest months of the year, and a sudden fall of temperature brings about generous rains. However, these thunderstorms are mostly local conditions, refreshing barely more than a two-mile radius, and thus it may happen that large stretches of land are parched by the drought, while adjoining areas may be drenched with liberal rains.

From conditions such as described, farmers and stockmen alike suffer. The creeks and rivers become dry, the grass in the pastures becomes scorched, the animals become poor from lack of grass and water, and, should the dearth of rain continue for several years, livestock is sure to die of starvation and thirst. As the herds cannot be disposed of or their natural increase stopped at will, the cattlemen are bound to swim with the current, as it were, and bear the consequences as well as they can. No human power or agency is adequate to battle successfully against nature and the elements.

Efforts made in San Antonio and throughout West Texas to produce rain artificially proved futile, although many were encouraged by the appropriation of state funds and by private contributions. Based upon the well-known fact that in war after great battles, where large quantities of explosives were employed, a few rainy days and even weeks would frequently result, the garrison at San Antonio received orders to send up balloons with dynamite bombs and make them explode in heavy masses of clouds. For weeks the sky was bombarded in this manner day and night, and in such a manner that admitted of little sleep. The results, however, did not come up to expectations. After strenuous bombardments another very interesting experiment was tried, namely, to force cold air into the heated air strata by steam-driven fans arranged in a tower built for this particular purpose. These experiments also failed because the air forced up did not remain cold enough on its way to the clouds but became heated as it ascended and expanded. Finally, the interested parties and sponsors were convinced that the only possible way to overcome these recurring dry periods was to utilize the subterranean watercourses, and much is now annually done in this respect.

Having said so much about the trials and tribulations of the cattleman, let us now see how the farmer fares in dry weather.

After he has planted the seed in the early spring, the absence of the required rainfall is the source of his greatest anxiety. In the ordinary course of events cottonseed should sprout one week after being planted. Corn requires a few days longer. When the soil is dry, the seed will not sprout and has to be replanted. The fields will soon be overrun with weeds even without rains, so they have to be hoed and plowed at more or less regular intervals, otherwise the growing seed cannot break through the parched soil. If no rain is forthcoming at the time the cotton is ready to bloom, the new-grown bolls fall to the ground. Later rains will effect a second growth of new bolls, but these are frequently destroyed by insects. A satisfactory corn crop can be obtained only if the plant receives a liberal rain during the tasseling period; if not, the plant becomes stunted and its stalks must be cut down and used as fodder.

In dry years the tillers of the soil turn to foodstuffs and grain, the seeds of which are imported from the arid regions of the globe and are able to withstand great droughts. Sorghum, kaffir corn, milo maize and Johnson grass come under the category of foodstuffs, but there is little market for these products, and the cost of transportation is so high compared with that of compressed cotton that it behooves the farmer and stockman to grow a supply necessary for his own stock.

It was in the eighties of the last century that stock-raising began to be carried on according to more scientific principles, and to give the layman an idea of a medium-sized ranch, I should like to add a short description of my Twin Sisters Ranch.

An area of about seven thousand acres was fenced by barbed wire nailed to cedar posts. About one hundred acres had been put in cultivation to supply the winter feed for the horses and such cattle as were sick or debilitated. Near the source of Simmons Creek log houses had been erected for the farmhands and cowboys. A sheepfold capable of accommodating fifteen hundred sheep during cold nights stood nearby, and one hundred additional acres were fenced in as a separate pasture for the saddle and draft horses because horses do not like to graze where sheep have been kept, nor do cattle like such grounds. Therefore, the sheep must be kept in separate pastures. The most profitable breed of sheep are the Spanish Merinos, as their wool is fine and commands a premium. Then, too, they can be grazed in pastures of inferior quality, with little water and plenty of weeds, as this kind of sheep prefers weeds to the best quality of grass. The maintenance of a herd of sheep was comparatively inexpensive, as they did not have to be fed during the winter months, for they would even eat the acorns on the ground. And the wages of the shepherds were reasonably low. A Mexican shepherd with two good dogs was able to drive the entire herd to the mountain pastures and return with them in the evening. The only time he needed help was during the ewing time, when our herd would increase to two thousand head. These Mexicans were very frugal—a wool blanket sufficed for their bed, and their breakfast consisted of bacon and cornbread. They partook of their principal meal in the evening after the return of the flock. This meal consisted of the brown, nutritious Mexican beans, which they placed on the coals of their campfire of the night before and would find cooked and ready to be served on their return in the afternoon. Mexican shepherds were trustworthy, and only once or twice a year did they desire to break their solitude to visit friends or make purchases at the nearest town. At a late hour at night they would sometimes visit the shepherds on other ranches maybe four or five miles away and indulge in music or card playing until almost morning, but punctually at the appointed time they would be back on the job and lead their flock again to the pasture.

I employed a few Negroes for field work and had no reason to be dissatisfied with their services but had to let them know their places. In general they were not given to gambling like the Mexicans but squandered their hard-earned money on finery and would share during their dances and amusements their provisions and hospitality with their invited neighbors. The younger Negroes were good horsemen and helped with the care of the cattle.

The cattle pastures had a sufficient supply of water. Besides abundant wells, the pumps of which were driven by windmills, the south side of the pastures was bounded for some miles by the Guadalupe River. The entire area was about eight miles in length and three miles wide. At a distance of about five miles from the main pasture, near my own residence, I had reserved a smaller pasture of six hundred acres for a small herd of English Red Polls. It comprised

about a hundred head of rich dark-red color, the offspring of imported stock. With the fine bulls bred from this herd I provided my
Twin Sisters Ranch; the others I sold to my neighbors who desired
to improve their breeds, at fancy prices. In a pasture of four thousand acres situated between Miller Creek and the Pedernales, eight
miles distant from my residence, I kept such animals as were intended for market, and these had to be kept separated from the
other herds. They amounted to five hundred head, and to fatten
them was an inexpensive matter. The formation of the ground was
calcareous; the water contained lime and after drinking it the cattle
were always hungry for salt. This circumstance saved us the trouble
of rounding them up. When we were ready to make an inspection,
all we had to do was to spread a few sacks of salt on the ground, and
the entire herd would come running to the spot. Many deep holes
were licked into the earth by the cattle, which goes to prove how
great was their desire and how urgent their need for salt in calcareous regions. On our Twin Sisters Ranch, we pastured eight hundred
head of mixed stock made up of cows, heifers, and grown steers
from three to five years old, in addition to a large herd of sheep. Half
the latter were fed on fodder during the winter and later shipped to
the markets in the north. The cattle managed to live in the open,
feeding on grass and weeds. Only during dry, cold winters were we
obliged to feed them. When times were especially hard we would
sometimes feed them on cactus leaves after their needles had been
removed by singeing.

During the warm summer months a plentiful supply of water is
far more necessary for livestock than feed, and cattle particularly
when deprived of water emaciate rapidly and lose their vitality.

In the year 1894 a moderate drought occurred, affecting the
springs and diminishing their output of water, and in the following
year there was hardly any rainfall. The Guadalupe River, in normal
times a swift and ample stream, was reduced to a string of waterholes; however, our wells still supplied their regular quantity of
water. From the small rings of the trees which we cut down I inferred that we were approaching one of those long dry periods previously described. I tried to protect myself from its injurious effects
in every conceivable way. I had several new wells drilled on our
ranch, and in addition to hay ordered from distant parts of the state,

I bought quantities of cottonseed for the impending period of stock feeding. We tried to cut down our stock by frequent sales, but the beef cattle soon became so poor that they were unable to walk the long way to the railroad loading station, especially after all the streams and watercourses between the ranch and the station had dried up.

With slender hopes we entered the winter of 1896. We expected to have some winter rains but were again disappointed. The big waterholes in the Guadalupe River near the Twin Sisters Ranch were entirely dry, and the bed of the river was nothing but a barren waste. Subsequently many of our weaker cattle died, yet we still hoped to save the larger part of our herd. After the Guadalupe had gone dry and the springs stopped flowing, even our wells furnished less water, and the ground became so scorched that good-sized trees withered and died. Deep clefts and fissures six feet deep opened and made rapid riding unsafe if not impossible. Every morning we hoped for the rain that passed over our heads in heavy clouds but never precipitated to refresh the arid lands.

It was a peculiarity of these regions that early in the morning a heavy dew would fall even during the most severe droughts, only to be immediately absorbed with the rising of the sun.

Many kinds of small animals—rabbits, birds, lizards, and snakes —do not have to have water at all as a matter of fact, as they can gain their sustenance from the dew on weeds and flowers. Among the larger animals only sheep can sustain themselves by drinking the dew from plants and grass, and in an emergency such as described, they were driven to the pastures long before sunrise. When the sun has dried the ground, the sheep seek the protection of the shade, where they rest until evening. In this way I have saved a whole flock of sheep without any loss. Their wool continued to grow and they remained in fairly good condition. But with cattle and horses it is entirely different. When water becomes scarce, they grow nervous and restless. They are ever on the move, running along fences in search of cooler places. Thus they spend their strength and the weaker animals are soon forced to lie down never to rise again. Once in this depleted condition they will stoutly refuse the best feed that may be placed before them, or to drink any water even when dying of thirst. Many of our finest animals we would raise to their feet by a hoisting contrivance, but they were too weak to stand or take feed or water, and, hiding in the deep brush, they would remain mute and motionless and welcome death with a calm indifference.

This is the time when the loathsome buzzards gather from everywhere and begin feeding on the expiring animals while there is still a spark of life in them. The eyes of the animals would be torn from their sockets. It was our sad task to save the poor beasts from this unnecessary torture by shooting them when the last hope was apparently gone. I was never able to understand why thousands of helpless creatures have to suffer so terribly before their final dissolution. It did not even pay to skin the animals, as their hides had become almost worthless. During such times and amidst such surroundings man becomes indifferent to any misfortune that may befall him, as it is beyond his power of comprehension why the forces of nature destroy in a few short years what they have helped to create. Under such circumstances the most cheerful and optimistic person grows dull and indifferent. Formerly my cowboys would go gaily about their appointed tasks, riding away with laughter in their hearts, but now when we would begin our unhappy labors, they were mute and taciturn, exchanging only the most commonplace remarks. Even our saddle horses seemed to be influenced by the general gloom.

I still cherished the hope of being able to fight my way through, and some banker friends who shared my hopes and ambitions furnished the means for buying hay from Kansas, a distance of a thousand miles, in order to save my cattle, but soon these means were exhausted; I had deeply involved myself in debt and there was little hope for an improvement in conditions. Of all the cattle placed in the Miller Creek pasture, only one-third survived. In the Twin Sisters pastures the number to survive was less than one-half. My sheep had suffered less, but the returns from their sale in the northern markets barely covered the cost of transportation. And equally unsatisfactory were the results of the sale of the Red Poll herd, which I had saved by the utmost exertions. As a result of the general droughts, all the remaining livestock was thrown on the market, and as the supply far exceeded the demand, trainloads of cattle brought only the most meager returns.

It was to be expected that this sinister situation would depre-

ciate the value of ranches and farms because all the breeders and
cattlemen had by this time incurred debts and were forced to sell
their valuable properties for meager considerations in order to meet
their most pressing obligations. I was one of the unfortunates who
had to face this very situation and was forced to sell my splendid
ranches for a paltry sum.

Everything in this world is subject to change. In the autumn of
1896, after the drought had spent its force, we were blessed with
magnificent rains, and in a few short months all the pastures flourished more beautifully than ever before. The grass grew luxuriantly,
cattle prices advanced constantly, and the new owners became inde-
pendently wealthy. Many of the former proprietors had lost their
spirit and initiative, while others turned to other branches of industry. Many banks had become insolvent and it was difficult to establish credit.

It was a trying time for me. My hair had grown a snowy white
within a brief two years, and my prospects for the future were dark
and discouraging indeed. At the age of forty-eight I had to begin
working anew for strangers, and I was so much tortured by the
thought of being a poor man among my old acquaintances, who had
accustomed themselves to seek my advice in many of their difficulties, that I resolved to leave Blanco County, which had been so dear
to my heart. This blow of misfortune was hard to bear, especially
when I thought of my family. My fine wife and I had married when
very young, and our union was blessed with twelve children, seven
sons and five daughters. I considered a good education the best gift
a father can bestow on his children, and as there were no higher
institutions of learning in Blanco County, I had sent some of our
children to schools away from home. My eldest sons had worked
hard and assisted me faithfully during the years of adversity and,
when confronted by the stern realities of life, had learned that many
difficulties can be overcome by courage and perseverance, but that it
is vain to battle against the superior powers of natural laws. I now
assembled my family and explained to them that we were entirely
destitute of means and had to begin anew our struggle for existence.
It was sad news to them, but they were not discouraged. I then and
there made up my mind to move to one of the small German settlements where I could give my smaller children an opportunity to

learn in a German school how to read and write the German language. And I strictly saw to it that our children used the German language in our home, and I now have the satisfaction of knowing that all of them are perfect in the use of the language so dear to us.

After I had given up my properties, I rode to the summit of the beautiful Twin Sisters mountains to take a last farewell of the wide expanse of land that I had called my own for twenty-five years, and where I had spent the best energies as well as the happiest days of my life. The early morning of my last visit was indeed gloomy. So were my thoughts. There in the distance I could see the houses of my former employees. The smoke curled up into the air from the fires on which these people were cooking their morning meal. I was now one of their own class and condition. Torturing doubts as to whether I still had the courage and energy to endure this kind of life or to lift myself to a higher sphere beset my soul. I went back in memory to the time I entered this country and reviewed my life in a series of mental pictures, showing all the advantages gained, all the losses sustained during this long interval, and proved that my life's work had not benefited myself alone, but also the land of my choice. I came to see how easily I had overcome all the obstacles and difficulties and how I had ever been ready and willing to help my neighbors and those who had been less fortunate than I.

While I was thus busily engaged with my thoughts, the sun rose gloriously above the horizon, gilding with its bright rays the beautiful landscape so well known to me and so dear to my heart. My courage rose with the rising sun, and I resolved to begin the struggle for a life worth living with renewed courage and energy. Animated by this thought I put my spurs to my horse, and singing with a glad voice the following passage from the "Beggar Student,"
"Fate, your worst now do.
I shall die or conquer you!"
I descended the mountains and began a new life.

"Ad Astra per Aspera"

(To the stars through difficulties)

I now moved to the little city of New Braunfels and became a life and fire insurance agent. It was a hard job for a sensitive man, the insurance business in those days being about on a par with a traveling book-agent. Such persons were looked down upon and their company was avoided rather than courted; however, I had to suppress my own feelings and pride, as the welfare of my family was at stake. I made barely enough money to keep the wolf from the door, as the saying goes. In those days it was a practical joke for the husband to give his wife as Christmas presents a new axe with which to chop wood and a garden hoe with which to work in the fields. This joke proved to be sad reality in our case.

I rented the little home of H. Babel and was just getting to a place where I could make a living when Mama became ill and remained in bed for several months until a serious operation relieved her. These were probably the hardest times we had to live through. No help for the sick and no means to pay for enough provisions to feed all the mouths. Day by day, I took the road behind my two sorrel horses to the neighboring towns to write insurance and tried to reach home after night hours to take care of poor Emily and Alex, who was also seriously ill. But the turn came and Emily got well and took care of the home and children.

There was never a time when I was not on the look-out for any opportunity to improve our situation. I finally heard of a large tract of land near New Braunfels that was to be sold, and I succeeded in getting the agency for the sale. After several weeks I found an

immigrant who had just arrived from the Rhineland and who possessed the necessary cash. I sold him the property for $30,000 and
this netted me $3,000 in commissions. With this sum I would have
been glad to start a small business of my own, as it did not appear
probable at the time that I would ever be able to engage in the
ranch business again, yet at the same time I longed to be my own
master once more.

I had gained considerable experience in handling machinery as
well as building mills, but my technical knowledge was not sufficient
to enable me to manage a machine shop. But, having a predilection
for machinery, I tried to improve my knowledge by spending every
spare minute studying various treatises on mechanics. After months
of study I applied for a position as salesman for the F. F. Collins
Manufacturing Company, a large machinery house in San Antonio.
My services were accepted, but more on account of my acquaintance than because of my knowledge of the business. My salary was
small, but the work afforded me an excellent opportunity to get acquainted with the most modern types of equipment, and after six
months spent as a traveling salesman, I was not only thoroughly
informed in all the branches of our business, but I had discovered
many weak spots in the management of the company's affairs. The
treatment accorded the firm's customers had made it unpopular
with the trade, and I was often advised by my friends and relatives
to establish a similar business of my own. Through several prosperous sales I had made on a commission basis I had accumulated a
rather substantial sum, about $7,000, in fact. However, this was not
enough to start a business with strong rivals in the field. I tried to
increase my capital by borrowing, which could be done by either
applying to the banks or by forming a new company.

Such a business as I planned required not only warehouses for
storing engines, windmills, piping, farm and ranch implements, but
a small plant where machinery could be repaired and where some
articles required by the trade could be manufactured. Under this
classification came brass cylinders for pumps, corn mills, and all
kinds of farm and ranch engines and irrigation supplies.

After awhile I made the acquaintance of a young Kentuckian,
Harry Gunther, who owned a small factory of this kind, and we
agreed to form a new company. He was to act as superintendent of

the factory and I was to furnish capital to the extent of $10,000, which was about equal to the value of his machinery. In addition to this I was to furnish the business with the required stock and act as general manager of the entire plant.

Up to this time my three eldest sons had had to earn their own living, and they gladly gave their small savings to their mother, who was an invalid for a long time and had to be given special care. My eldest son managed a small country store for the owner. The second son was employed as bookkeeper in a cottonseed oil mill, and the youngest of the three was apprenticed to a photographer. I was able to employ my sons and have them at home again, a circumstance which inspired me to greater endeavors, as everybody enjoys working for his own loved ones more than working for others.

In the beginning our stock was small; however, we were trusted with the representation of northern factories, which greatly increased our sales. From the proceeds of our business we purchased new tools for the factory, especially a large steam hammer. *We had rented a building on Military Plaza for the sales end of the business. The first help I employed were Willy Brooks and his father. Mr. Cowdry became our bookkeeper and Matt Gotts, the shipping clerk. We now were making great strides to success and needed more money, so we took in Ben Stribling as a third partner, who also furnished $10,000. We changed the name from Krueger & Gunther to the San Antonio Machine & Supply Co. (1899), making a stock company of it with $50,000 paid in capital.*

Our business prospects brightened but our difficulties increased in proportion. My partner, Mr. Gunther, had been thrown from a horse years before and sustained an injury of the skull, and now long after the misfortune his brain became affected to such a degree that at times he was wholly irrational and irresponsible both as to his words and his actions, and I was compelled to superintend the factory and repair work and gain the required insight into these branches of the business. Our business flourished and soon attracted the attention of rivals and competitors who were stronger financially than we were. In time many of their customers became dissatisfied and began to favor us with their business. A hard fight for supremacy resulted and lasted for two years. Eventually we won out and had the satisfaction of taking over our rivals and annexing their plant to our own. *In 1905, we increased our capital to $100,000 and bought out our main competitors for $42,000. In 1913, our capital was increased to $300,000 and we began to build the new plant on Center Street on the Southern Pacific. The year 1916 found us with $450,000; 1919 with $600,000 capital; and 1920 with $1,000,000 capital and $645,000 surplus.*

Naturally I arranged for my sons who intended to devote their energies to our business to acquire a thorough knowledge of the particular branch they had chosen for themselves. Willy, my eldest son, succeeded in recovering the Twin Sisters Ranch, together with the cotton gin and mill which were my former properties, and he now enjoys bright prospects for a prosperous future. Max, my second son, established his own business in San Antonio, which he later sold to become manager of the San Antonio branch of a large manufacturing corporation. Paul, my third son, I had intended to be my successor, but during the World War he succumbed to a severe attack of the influenza that prevailed at that time throughout the country. Lee, my fourth son, went to Mexico while still a young man to study conditions and opportunities in that country and to master the Spanish language. He is now vice-president of our company and specializes in the sale of pumping and irrigation machinery. My fifth son, Walter, possessed remarkable talent for all things pertaining to and connected with mechanics. He attended the Agricultural and Mechanical College of Texas and was afterward employed in the great Atlas Engine Works at Indianapolis, thus combining theoretical knowledge with practical training. He is now manager of our factory. Carl, my sixth son, is a graduate of the Texas Agricultural and Mechanical College and entered military life during the World War, leaving the army with the rank of major of the 82nd Field Artillery to take the place of my deceased son Paul. He served as my personal representative during my absence and now manages the affairs of the company to my entire satisfaction. Alex, our youngest son, is in charge of our engineering department.

All my sons and five daughters are married. The reader of these reminiscences will doubtless agree with me that it was a difficult task to rear so large a family and give every member of it an opportunity to attend the best schools and become successful and proficient in their respective vocations. The fact that I have been able to do this for my children consoles and comforts me in my declining years with the conviction that I have tried to do my duty, and there is no greater reward and satisfaction than this thought.

The next twenty years of my life I dedicated to the gradual enlargement and expansion of our business and plant, and I am happy to relate that it grew even to greater proportions until now it is one of the largest and best establishments of its kind in Texas.

It was never our aim to limit the business of our plant to the manufacture of a few articles for immediate demand, but to be governed by the particular needs of the community. To this end we discontinued making many articles formerly manufactured and introduced newer and improved kinds of machinery and equipment. Our business now is principally the building of oil engines and pumps for irrigation purposes, drilling machinery for oil and water wells, steam engines, boilers for distilling crude oil, and special makes of pumping engines. For agricultural purposes we make chiefly cotton gin machinery. Sources of perennial joy to me were our iron and brass foundries, which were equipped with the most modern and efficient improvements and machinery.

During my business career, even in the earlier years, I came in contact with prominent manufacturers and bankers, and it was often regrettable to realize that while many of them were excellent in all things pertaining to their own particular business activities, they were sadly lacking in many of the essentials of a well-rounded and general education. Showing a lively concern in their own special branch of industry and finance, they seemed to have lost all interest and became dull when in the course of our conversation some subject was touched upon that lay beyond their particular sphere. For their recreation many of these gentlemen chose golf, which was an ever-recurring topic of conversation. The esteem and affectionate friendship I met with in their society were sources of great joy and satisfaction to me, and I experience the most extreme pleasure in stating here that my confidence in my own efficiency was greatly strengthened by my association with these gentlemen. It is my firm belief that only he who trusts in himself can succeed in any great business venture, provided this self-reliance does not degenerate into arrogance and boastfulness.

At an early date I became acquainted with the directors of the great Steel Trust, and I am happy to say that I was always cordially received and at home in their company. Having read a great deal about the ways of caring and providing for laborers and their families, introduced by Krupp in Essen, Germany, I often conversed about this theme with the gentlemen at the head of the steel works in Pittsburgh. I took a lively interest myself in every step calculated to bring us nearer to social and economic equality and soon found an opportunity to get the president of the Steel Trust interested in similar endeavors. During my next visit to Germany I was for several weeks a guest of the Krupp Works and minutely studied their system of caring for their employees. I was not only able to get a clear insight into their methods and arrangements for the care of invalids and the aged and their system of pensioning their personnel, but the directors were kind enough to provide me with a great number of pamphlets and other literature relating to these subjects. Today, after many years, I have the satisfaction of seeing my efforts in this direction transformed into working realities. Where not more than twenty years ago an army of a quarter of a million workingmen was treated like slaves by the largest steel concern in the world, paying their employees liberally indeed but making no provision whatever for their bodily and spiritual welfare, there now stands an institution of the highest excellence, capable of being the prototype for all similar institutions yet to come. There are schools for the immigrants where they are taught to read and speak the native tongue; their hospitals represent the last word in medicine and hygiene; night schools are provided to give the children of the workers opportunities to improve themselves in all branches of learning. Public playgrounds for children and adults and public baths bordering on luxury may be found in their various industrial settlements and communities. All the employees are given an opportunity to become partners in the great enterprises by buying stock below its par value and on the credit of the company. At the head of the Steel Trust now is the younger generation, new blood, and some of them well know who it was that gave the first impulse to all these radical changes, and it is some satisfaction to be conscious of having been conducive to the realization of this wholesome and beneficent idea, even though those who reap its benefits do not even know the name of its originator.

During the past fifteen years I have traveled much, and many an interesting journey offered an opportunity to compare the conditions and mode of living in our own United States with those of other countries and nations. As I never lost my pleasure and interest in stock-raising, I visited during an extended journey the republics of South America, especially the Argentine republic. That country is our greatest competitor in providing the world with cheap meat, and when traveling over its endless plains from Buenos Aires to Mendoza, the diligent observer becomes convinced that Argentina will be in later years our superior in this branch of the industry. During a ride of a thousand miles not a single rock was to be seen. The pampas are as flat and level as a table. The cattle business of that country is largely in the hands of Scotchmen who are amply provided with English money. These breeders do not suffer so much from dry and rainy periods, and their lands are generally cheaper and the taxes infinitely lower than ours. I have often noticed that great patches of alfalfa alternate with some of the native grasses, and this fact saves the breeders from the necessity of using fodder to fatten their cattle for the market. As water can be found everywhere on those vast plains at a depth of from ten to twenty feet, the grass and alfalfa roots can reach moisture easily and need not be replanted for years.

How different is life on a ranch in Argentina from that in Texas. The half-breeds (mestizos) and natives resemble our Mexicans in size and color, but their habitations and garments are superior to those of our own peons. The horses of the ranches are nearly all of Spanish blood. The saddles of the "gauchos" or Argentine cowboys would be exceedingly uncomfortable for a Texan. Without a solid saddletree, they are so wide that the knees must be kept far apart. In place of our lasso with a loop which is thrown around the horn, they have the ends of their ropes provided with several iron balls (bolas), which, after being thrown, encircle the hind legs of the animal by centrifugal force, thus causing it to fall. Pampas cattle seemed less wild than our Texas steers, and the gauchos less skillful than our cowboys. This difference in their working qualities may be accounted for by their saddles which have only one stirrup, and a very short one at that. But I observed one decided advantage in their method of loading cattle on railroad cars. In the United States every car of a cattle train must be loaded separately, while in Argentina the cars are so connected that the beeves after entering the last car can move on through the entire train, thus saving the shipper much time and trouble. To provide the cattle on trains with food and water for refreshment en route to market was a thing unknown to the Argentinians ten years ago, or at least I never saw any such arrangement.

Great slaughter houses such as we have in Chicago, St. Louis, and Kansas City have been established there and are managed by our American packers—Swift & Company, Armour, and others. Apart from their great local output, huge quantities of frozen meat are sent to Europe by the shipload and sold for less than the home products. But the sale of the beeves in the stockyards is handled in an entirely different manner than ours. On my first visit early in the morning I saw about seven thousand steers which had been unloaded during the night. They were distributed among several different pens in such a way that every pen contained from ten to twenty-five animals. Nowhere did I see the cattle inspected as to their health, although I saw about twenty steers suffering from bigjaw and hoof-and-mouth disease to such a degree that would have made their sale impossible in this country. The purchasers began to bid on the steers in the pens, but the animals thus sold were not even weighed, consequently the new owners were unable to estimate the profits gained by such purchase. Besides the wholesale buyers, the local butchers also purchased small numbers of lowgrade beeves to be sold to the poorer classes of the Buenos Aires population, which numbers more than one million. These animals were immediately killed in the slaughter houses established near the cattle pens and the waste materials left on the ground for the beggars, whose wrangling for their share of the refuse reminded me of the fights of the Texas buzzards over the carcasses of stricken animals.

After this digression to South America, I want to ask my readers to return with me to our own Texas.

Texas and Its Resources

MANY of my friends and acquaintances may desire to have the Lone Star State described as it is today, and in order to compare the past with the present, I shall include a brief description of Texas as we now know it.

Texas is the largest state in the Union. Its area is as large as Germany and Switzerland combined. It is blessed with a wonderful climate and destined to surpass all the other states of the Union in products and population. Even at the present day one-third of all the cotton produced in the United States is produced in Texas.

Also in the breeding and growing of livestock Texas outranks all other states. Maize, grain, oranges, and fruits of the temperate zone are grown in regions where the climate is best adapted to these products. In an area as large as Texas all kinds of climate prevail. In the southern part of the state the climate is almost tropical, in the northern part it is temperate, and in the mountainous regions it is cool, but in our blessed country, like everywhere else on the globe, there are disadvantages to offset some of our advantages. For instance, the long droughts that cause inestimable havoc. Sometimes there will be no rainfall for years, and the consequences are poor crops and no grass, which cause the cattle to become emaciated and unfit for sale. In addition to this we have the night frosts likely to occur from October to April, following the cold northers that suddenly come on us, injuring the young cotton and stunting the sprouting corn, which compels the farmer to replant his crops. These newly planted crops are in turn treated rather harshly by nature, the heat in May and June affecting them unfavorably. Poor crops again mean a diminished purchasing power for the farmers and stockmen, and this in turn affects banks and business concerns generally because a large number of the planters and cattlemen operate on a credit basis and are not only not able to pay their maturing bills but are unable to finance themselves until the next crop. This untoward situation is alleviated somewhat by the fact that real crop failures generally affect only restricted parts of the state, while other sections may not suffer at all. The climatic conditions throughout the country vary, one part experiencing an absence of moisture while other sections have too much. By and large, the western part of Texas is subject to droughts, while the eastern part has a super-abundance of rain.

For this reason more cotton is raised in the western part because the leaves of this plant take some nourishment from the air, while the northern part of Texas is more adapted to the growing of grain and cereals, especially oats and wheat, the roots of which get their moisture from the soil. This latter process is greatly facilitated by the copious rainfalls in these sections.

However, there are two ways by which nature equalizes the effects of these extreme climatic conditions. In vast areas of western Texas, subject to a dearth of rain, artesian water can be easily obtained by drilling deep wells, and water from these can be used for irrigation. These water strata are generally encountered at a depth of about seven hundred feet below the surface. An excellent example of the enormous pressure of the subterranean waters is afforded by the artesian wells of San Antonio and throughout Southwest Texas. Within an area of not more than one acre there are fourteen wells, each drilled to a depth of seven hundred feet. These wells raise the enormous quantity of twelve million gallons of water daily to the surface without the aid of pumps, and this amount of water is sufficient for a city of two or three hundred thousand population. The average diameter of these wells is ten inches, but a well of the same depth with a diameter of twenty inches near San Antonio has a daily output of twelve million gallons of water. As far as I know, there is only one other well in all the world capable of such a large volume. It is the famous artesian well in Paris, France, which, with a greater diameter and greater depth, produces fifteen million gallons of water daily. This well has, however, materially decreased its output in late years. In addition to this rich artesian vein there is abundant water to be encountered at depths ranging from forty to two hundred feet, but it has to be hoisted to the surface by pumps to be used for irrigation purposes. Besides all this artesian water in the region of San Antonio, there are enormous deposits of petroleum waiting to be brought to the surface from its subterranean caverns. The greatest quantities of this commodity are found, it is true, at depths varying from two thousand to four thousand feet, and therefore are difficult to get, but even at the present time Texas abounds in thousands of shallow oil wells at depths of one hundred to seven hundred feet and equals in this respect the best producing areas in America.

I thought it necessary to give this description of modern Texas, as it still is to a great number of Europeans and even Americans as much of a "terra incognita" as any part of Central Africa. Many people believe that Texas is largely peopled by cowboys and Indians, and a few prospective visitors arm themselves for defense after they have crossed the border of our state.

The great changes a new country can undergo within the space of fifty years is truly miraculous and indeed almost incredible. When I entered Texas, the eastern part of the state was densely covered with pine forests, the long-leaf pine being one of our most valuable products. Today these pine forests have vanished, completely ruined by the exploitation of mercenary parties, and the poor sandy soil where they flourished has become practically worthless, as it is too barren for agriculture. Adjoining those formerly wooded regions in the southern part of the state, down to the Gulf of Mexico, where in olden days the poor sedge-grass prevailed, are to be found the great rice fields and sulfur deposits of Texas. There, too, the first oil wells of the state were drilled, enriching, it is true, a large number of people, but impoverishing others. The oil wells on the famous "Spindletop" gave rise to many profitable explorations for oil in other parts of the state and nation. It was on Spindletop that oil gushers first made their appearance. A gusher is a deep well, on the oil of which such pressure is exerted by gas that the oil bursts high up into the air. It was a frequent occurrence that the heavy wooden derricks about eighty feet in height, by which the drills and steel cables are passed into the well, were entirely demolished by the torrent of oil, and as long as there is any gas pressure, it is difficult to control the wells or to stop the flow of oil. In cases like this the oil is directed into huge reservoirs constructed of loose earth, previous to conducting it into steel tanks having a capacity of about fifty-five thousand barrels. There is usually some gas where oil is found, but in some locations where only gas is found, it develops a terrific pressure. For example, it was impossible to confine the deep gas well brought in at White Point, near Corpus Christi. Through careless handling the gas became ignited, and its immense flames continued to burn for months. In ever-repeating eruptions, it belched forth rocks, earth, and mud, thus forming a deep crater of several hundred feet dimensions. Beaumont, Breckenridge, and Wichita Falls were famous for their oil gushers, and wherever oil was found in large quantities little towns would spring up almost overnight, and giant pipelines were built to convey the oil to the nearest railway station, from which solid trainloads of tank cars would be used to transport the oil all over the civilized world. To be able to transport this oil by ocean-going vessels, pipelines six to twelve inches in diameter were laid from the North Texas oil fields to the Gulf of Mexico, and in the same way natural gas was piped over long distances to the cities, thereby diminishing the cost of domestic and industrial fuel. San Antonio receives its supply of natural gas from wells one hundred miles away.

There are large oil fields with shallow wells in many parts of Texas, especially south of San Antonio. They are provided with pumping contrivances which force the oil to the surface. Many of these wells are so connected that the power for the pumps can be supplied by a central station. In all places where oil is found refineries are established and crude oil is distilled and changed into illuminating and lubricating oils and gasoline. Great oil centers like Beaumont and Houston largely owe their rapid growth to the oil industry. Houston grew rapidly after the unfortunate city of Galveston was devastated by one of these recurring flood-storms of the Gulf, in which thousands of people were drowned. The Houston of today boasts of more than a quarter of a million population. The bayous intervening between Houston and Galveston have been deepened, putting Houston in possession of an excellent inland harbor, from which large quantities of cotton, cotton by-products, oil, lumber, and grain are exported.

The harbor of Galveston, fifty miles from Houston, was protected from flood damages by building a granite wall fifteen feet high. Houston, being a railroad center, has become one of the most active commercial cities of Texas.

The entire country west of Galveston along the Gulf to Corpus Christi has developed from a poor grazing land into a rich farming country which seems particularly well adapted to the cultivation of cotton. It is very probable that the salty sea air enhances the yield of the crops. The city of Corpus Christi was subsidized by the federal and state governments for the purpose of getting a safe and adequate harbor which will enable western Texas to become independent of the other harbors of the state.

In this region the "Fata Morgana" so often described by travelers in northern Africa is a frequent, and in summertime, a daily occurrence. These mirages present ever the same picture of South Texas, a large inland lake about two to five miles away, from which the tops of the trees seem to rise. When the spectator approaches any nearer, the mirage begins to recede and finally melts away. These phenomena were an ordinary occurrence near the little town of Bishop, Texas, and the inhabitants were fond of playing jokes on strangers unacquainted with this peculiarity of the country. One day a party of tourists stopped at the hotel in Bishop and asked for details about the large and beautiful lake which they had noticed just beyond the town. They were especially curious to know if it contained many varieties of fish and even asked permission to camp on its shore. Their requests were granted for a fee of a dollar each, but they never reached the lake though they imagined they could see it clear and distinct in the distance.

West of Corpus Christi down to the Rio Grande River extend the immense ranches of the King and Kenedy families. The King Ranch has an area of one million acres. There are many other princely estates in Texas where fine breeds of cattle are raised. The residences of these cattle kings may well be called castles on account of their distinctive architectural style and the many conveniences and improvements with which they are provided.

For the past fifteen years repeated efforts have been made to subdivide these large estates and cut them up into small, productive farms. There is room for a hundred thousand small farmers, each of whom could acquire an area of one hundred acres.

The most astonishing change, however, has been wrought with the lands along the Rio Grande River, which forms the boundary line between Texas and Mexico. From the city of Brownsville, situated about thirty miles from the mouth of the Rio Grande, which empties into the Gulf, to Rio Grande City, less than a hundred miles to the northwest, the intervening territory was an impenetrable wilderness twenty-five years ago. The country was not even suitable for pasturage, as the cacti several feet high were shunned by man and beast alike. Now the country has been transformed within a short time into a veritable paradise. This southernmost part of the state is free from frosts, an advantage which makes it productive not only of all the crops of the temperate zone, but also of tropical fruits and vegetables. It was a herculean task indeed to clear this country of its cactus plants, brambles, and roots, but the land was fertile, consisting of rich, alluvial soil accumulated by the many inundations of the river, which extends to a total length of fifteen hundred miles. The Rio Grande River contains so much water that giant pumping stations have been erected on its banks to irrigate that wonderful expanse of rich soil. Where luxuriant cactus plants formerly reared their heads there now flourish beautiful groves of oranges and grapefruit, and it is said the Rio Grande Valley citrus fruits have never been equaled in taste and quality. Cotton also grows profusely in the Valley, likewise broomcorn, onions, spinach, cabbage, and cauliflower, the latter ripening at an early date and shipped to northern markets during January and February. Later the different kinds of melons are shipped, also beans and peas, and these early shipments prove highly profitable to the growers. Within the short space of only a few years a dozen cities have sprung up in the Rio Grande Valley. Being new, these cities make a favorable impression on visitors. The streets are lined with beautiful palm trees, the public buildings are large and permanently built, and the homes reflect pride and prosperity.

The grand prairies of Central Texas with their beautiful wildflowers had to give way to agriculture, at least as far as the quality and condition of the soil permitted. There, far away in northern Texas, are produced the bumper crops, while wheat and other grains prosper in the northwestern part of the state.

In western Texas, the German population is on the increase, aided by natural fecundity as well as by immigration. Being more or less independent, the German farmer usually combines stock-raising with farming. Being practical people, they are unwilling to place all their chances on a single crop, and they reason that if one crop proves to be a failure, the sale of livestock will make up the deficit. In the western part of Texas cattle-raising is carried on according to improved methods, and finer stock is bred than in former times. The average ranchman of the present day has also gone in somewhat for raising sheep and goats, as the wool and mohair bring substantial returns at the minimum cost of production.

Retrospect – San Saba and the Indians

AND what became of beautiful San Saba? It can hardly be recognized any more by a man who called it his home fifty years ago. By numerous livestock, the fine expanse of grassland has been trampled over and the sand thus released washed into the river, making it a shallow and dirty stream. The big springs long ago stopped flowing, and the lands formerly clad with forests of stately pecan trees are planted with cotton and corn. Since the country was traversed by the railroad, its population has increased and little San Saba, where I built the twelfth residence the town could boast of, now proudly calls itself a middle-sized city. Its present-day inhabitants know nothing about those hardy pioneers who first made its civilization possible. It differs no longer from any other small Texas town. The sources of romance and poetry have vanished with the Indian and the free and independent spirit of former days. Those who were my companions and contemporaries have departed this life, and no one remains who knew or remembers me.

For the sake of those of my readers who may be curious to know what became of the Indian tribes which peopled this country in days gone by, and who fought a stubborn but losing fight against the encroachments of the white man, I wish to add the following explanation.

The Comanche Indians became tired of being constantly harassed by the United States military forces. With the advent of railroad and telegraph lines, which made their suppression much easier, the Indians left their old homes and sought and found new ones in Mexico on the banks of the Sabinas River. There they had no more opportunities for marauding and stealing, as the Indians who were their neighbors were their equals in every way. The Indian has never learned to work regularly and systematically. The women still attend to the little gardens where they raise a little corn, and the warriors indulge in hunting. They possess a few cattle, and I have often noticed them at the railway stations near Sabinas selling pearls and moccasins made of deerskin.

The Apaches are becoming extinct. In their encounters with frontiersmen in New Mexico many of them were killed. After they had maintained peace for a few years, they revolted again under their chief Geronimo. Under his leadership the Indians of Camp San Carlos and Camp Apache joined their forces in the fall of 1885 and committed a series of murders among peaceful ranch people. Immediately after these crimes several companies of the 4th Cavalry Regiment led by Indian scouts took up their trail under the command of Captain Allen Smith, and a long guerrilla war began, which terminated when Geronimo, after months of bloody fighting, surrendered to Lieutenant Gatewood. All the Apache prisoners were transferred to San Antonio and confined within the military post of this city. After a time they were transported to Florida, where most of them succumbed to the moist and unwonted climate. The few remaining Apaches who were scattered over New Mexico were taken into custody and settled on an Indian reservation fifteen miles from Cloudcroft. There I paid them a visit in 1918 and found the arrangement of the agency just mentioned excellent and practical. It was on a high plateau, seven thousand feet above sea level, with beautiful valleys abounding with springs and streams and covered with fine grasses. The mountains are clad with a growth of splendid pine trees, and the entire scenery much resembles some parts of Thuringia or the German Harz Mountains. The largest building of the reservation was the hospital. There were administration buildings, warehouses, a small schoolhouse, and dwellings designed for the Indians, but they could not be induced to live in them. Nearly every member of the tribe had become tubercular. Of 130 families, only 90 members were living when I visited them, and within a few years at the most the last of the Apaches will have vanished from the American continent, if they have not already done so.

At the Indian agency proper I saw only a few Apaches, all of whom were sick. During my conversation with the superintendent I witnessed a spectacle that would have been ridiculous had it not been so pathetic. Two Indian squaws riding a small pony came galloping up to get the provision rations apportioned to them. Both were old and wrinkled; their hair was disheveled and apparently had not been touched by a comb in many a moon. Both were without shoes or stockings, and their bodies down to the knees were covered with dirty rags. But the heads of these women were adorned with hats of the most modern fashion and trimmed with artificial flowers. While one of them handled the reins, the other held a big silk parasol of a very deep red over their heads, although the sun was not shining.

I visited the surrounding country on horseback to learn for myself how far civilization had advanced within forty years among those Indians, and soon found some of their tepees, which are small round tents covered with skins and rags. In front of the first tent an old Indian mother was sitting, surrounded by a number of little children, naked of course, and on the heads of whom she was diligently hunting for the ever-present vermin. As I approached she retreated into her tent and could not be prevailed on to say a single word. With that stoical indifference which is characteristic of the Indian, mother and children stared at me with their black pearly eyes, but the filth and stench soon forced me back into the open air. At the next tent I experienced the same treatment, but I had already seen enough to become convinced that there was neither change nor help possible for that miserable remnant of a once-brave and numerous tribe, and that soon its last representative would be gone forever.

The next morning, after my return to Cloudcroft, I noticed that the tent I had visited the afternoon before had been removed. I rode back to see what had become of it, and the trail I found in the grass disclosed to me the entire story. The Indians had lashed to the saddle on the only pony they possessed a few long poles, the ends of which trailed on the ground behind the horse, and folded up their ragged tent and packed it on the poles. After the entire family had sat down on it, the father led the pony away to raise the tepee on a spot perhaps miles from its former place, where no inquisitive paleface could molest them.

I beg leave now to finish my story, having told all my peculiar experiences. My later life does not differ essentially from that of any other businessman and is, I presume, well known to my many friends in Texas and elsewhere.

Conclusion

IN bringing this narrative to a conclusion, I should like to make a few parting observations. I have tried faithfully to describe in these chapters the life and fortunes of a German immigrant. Some of my readers who are unacquainted with me personally and my character may think that I have occasionally obtruded myself, as it were, too much into the limelight. But I can assure them that I was far from any such vainglorious idea. All I have wished to prove was the simple truth that no obstacle is too great, but that it can be overcome by courage, perseverance, and the use of those gifts which the creator has implanted within us. No man, therefore, need despair in this blessed country of ours, even in the depth of poverty, for a brighter and better fortune may be in store for him if he only tries to grasp the opportunity and knows how to hold on to it.

In this connection I think it worthwhile to give, by way of saying farewell, a word of advice to prospective immigrants. If young people wish to see the world and settle in foreign parts, let them do so. They will be quick to learn the language and in adapting themselves to new conditions and surroundings, but for those advanced in years I do not consider it a wise policy to change their home. They hardly ever learn the language of the new country and are forgetful of the fact that persons unable to talk the language are considered strangers by the natives and actually remain strangers the rest of their lives. Moreover, they generally stick to their old ideas and customs with an obstinate and pertinacious love and are prone to censure foreign institutions which they cannot understand and do not care to understand. In fact, anything and everything that does not measure up to their home standards makes them unhappy and dissatisfied. The saddest consequence, however, is the fact that frequently the children of immigrants grow ashamed of the father and mother who cannot converse fluently in the new tongue which they speak so easily themselves. Their filial love seems to decrease in proportion to their sense of their own refinement and superiority, and old family ties grow weaker.

If I have succeeded in interesting my readers by pleasantly filling in some of their leisure hours; if I have been able to inspire some of the younger generation with that indomitable courage that is indispensable for a successful struggle against the adversities of life; if I have induced some of the aged to remain in the land of their fathers and be content with existing home conditions; and, finally, if I have succeeded in painting a truthful and accurate picture of the good old days that are no more, and of our grand old state of Texas; then I can lay down my pen and say goodbye to my readers with the satisfaction of a man who has accomplished his task and performed a good and meritorious work.

Index

CPSIA information can be obtained
at www.ICGtesting.com
Printed in the USA
LVHW031355220821
695729LV00003B/267